# THIS LITTLE EARTH

by Jes

# SAMUEL FRENCH

Copyright © 2025 by Jessica Norman
Cover artwork © 2025 by Jed Berry
All Rights Reserved

*THIS LITTLE EARTH* is fully protected under the copyright laws of the British Commonwealth, including Canada, the United States of America, and all other countries of the Copyright Union. All rights, including professional and amateur stage productions, recitation, lecturing, public reading, motion picture, radio broadcasting, television, online/digital production, and the rights of translation into foreign languages are strictly reserved.

ISBN 978-0-573-00095-9

concordtheatricals.co.uk
concordtheatricals.com

---

**FOR AMATEUR PRODUCTION ENQUIRIES**

UNITED KINGDOM AND WORLD
EXCLUDING NORTH AMERICA
licensing@concordtheatricals.co.uk
020-7054-7298

Each title is subject to availability from Concord Theatricals, depending upon country of performance.

---

CAUTION: Professional and amateur producers are hereby warned that *THIS LITTLE EARTH* is subject to a licensing fee. The purchase, renting, lending or use of this book does not constitute a licence to perform this title(s), which licence must be obtained from the appropriate agent prior to any performance. Performance of this title(s) without a licence is a violation of copyright law and may subject the producer and/or presenter of such performances to penalties. Both amateurs and professionals considering a production are strongly advised to apply to the appropriate agent before starting rehearsals, advertising, or booking a theatre. A licensing fee must be paid whether the title is presented for charity or gain and whether or not admission is charged.

This work is published by Samuel French, an imprint of Concord Theatricals Ltd.

The Professional Rights in this play are controlled by United Agents Ltd, 12-26 Lexington St, London W1F 0LE.

No one shall make any changes in this title for the purpose of production. No part of this book may be reproduced, stored in a retrieval system, scanned, uploaded, or transmitted in any form, by any means, now known or yet to be invented, including mechanical, electronic, digital, photocopying, recording, videotaping, or otherwise, without the prior written permission of the publisher. No one shall share this title, or part of this title, to any social media or file hosting websites.

The moral right of Jessica Norman to be identified as author of this work has been asserted in accordance with Section 77 of the Copyright, Designs and Patents Act 1988.

### USE OF COPYRIGHTED MUSIC

A licence issued by Concord Theatricals to perform this play does not include permission to use the incidental music specified in this publication. In the United Kingdom: Where the place of performance is already licensed by the PERFORMING RIGHT SOCIETY (PRS) a return of the music used must be made to them. If the place of performance is not so licensed then application should be made to PRS for Music (www.prsformusic.com). A separate and additional licence from PHONOGRAPHIC PERFORMANCE LTD (www.ppluk.com) may be needed whenever commercial recordings are used. Outside the United Kingdom: Please contact the appropriate music licensing authority in your territory for the rights to any incidental music.

### USE OF COPYRIGHTED THIRD-PARTY MATERIALS

Licensees are solely responsible for obtaining formal written permission from copyright owners to use copyrighted third-party materials (e.g., artworks, logos) in the performance of this play and are strongly cautioned to do so. If no such permission is obtained by the licensee, then the licensee must use only original materials that the licensee owns and controls. Licensees are solely responsible and liable for clearances of all third-party copyrighted materials, and shall indemnify the copyright owners of the play(s) and their licensing agent, Concord Theatricals Ltd., against any costs, expenses, losses and liabilities arising from the use of such copyrighted third-party materials by licensees.

### IMPORTANT BILLING AND CREDIT REQUIREMENTS

If you have obtained performance rights to this title, please refer to your licensing agreement for important billing and credit requirements.

### NOTE

This edition reflects a rehearsal draft of the script and may differ from the final production.

*THIS LITTLE EARTH* was first produced by 3 hearts canvas and Izzy Carney, and was first performed at Arcola Theatre on 22 October 2025. The cast and creative team were as follows:

**HONEY** . . . . . . . . . . . . . . . . . . . . . . . . . . . . . . . . . . . . . . . . . . . . . . Fanta Barrie
**CHRISTOPHER** . . . . . . . . . . . . . . . . . . . . . . . . . . . . . . . . . Ross O'Donnellan

Playwright . . . . . . . . . . . . . . . . . . . . . . . . . . . . . . . . . . . . . . . . . Jessica Norman
Director . . . . . . . . . . . . . . . . . . . . . . . . . . . . . . . . . . . . . . . . . Imy Wyatt Corner
Producer . . . . . . . . . . . . . . . . . . . . . . . . . . . . . . . . . . . . . . . . . . . . . Izzy Carney
Producer . . . . . . . . . . . . . . . . . . . . . . . . . . . . . . . . . . . . . . . . . . 3 hearts canvas
Set and Costume Designer . . . . . . . . . . . . . . . . . . . . . . . . . . . . . . . . Cat Fuller
Light and Projection Designer . . . . . . . . . . . . . . . . . . . . . Hugo Dodsworth
Sound Designer . . . . . . . . . . . . . . . . . . . . . . . . . . . . . . . . . . . . . . . . . Jamie Lu
Movement Director . . . . . . . . . . . . . . . . . . . . . . . . . . . . . . . . . . . . . Hamza Ali
Stage Manager . . . . . . . . . . . . . . . . . . . . . . . . . . . . . . . . . . . . . Hannah Gillett
Production Manager . . . . . . . . . . . . . . . . . . . . . . . . . . . . . . Daniel Steward
Development Director . . . . . . . . . . . . . . . . . . . . . . . . . . . . . . . . Jess Edwards

**Arcola Theatre** produces daring, high-quality theatre in the heart of East London. We commission and premiere exciting, original works alongside rare gems of world drama and bold new productions of classics. We work with creatives from across the globe, acting as a platform for emerging and established artists, providing them space to grow, explore and refine their craft. Our socially engaged, international programme champions diversity, challenges the status quo, and stages trailblazing productions for everyone.

As part of our commitment to supporting the diversity of the theatre ecosystem, every year, we offer 26 weeks of free rehearsal space to culturally diverse and refugee artists; and our Participation department creates thousands of creative opportunities for the people of Hackney and beyond. Our community companies include Arcola Mental Health Company, Arcola 50+, Queer Collective, Sawa our refugee and migrant company, Arcola Academy and Arcola Youth Theatre. Our pioneering environmental initiatives are award-winning and aim to make Arcola the world's first carbon-neutral theatre.

Arcola has won awards including the UK Theatre Award for Promotion of Diversity, The Stage Award for Sustainability, the Off West End Award for Special Achievement, and the Peter Brook Empty Space Award.

## The Team

**Artistic Director**
Mehmet Ergen

**Deputy Artistic Director & Executive Producer**
Leyla Nazli

**General Manager / Participation Manager**
Charlotte Croft

**Producer / Artistic Associate**
Katharine Farmer

**Press Officer / Production Assistant**
Sadie Pearson

**Operations Managers**
Catriona Tait and Carmen Keeley Foster

**Finance Manager**
Steve Haygreen

**Marketing Manager**
Sarah Colson

**Marketing Coordinator**
Ella Muir

**Participation Coordinator**
Aoife Beaumont

**Trustees**
Andrew Cripps (Chair), Naz Yeni (Vice Chair), Ben Todd, Gabriel Gbadamosi, Abdullah Tercanli, Dr Graham Cooley

With grateful thanks to our Front of House, Technical and Bar teams, as well as all of our Supporters and Volunteers. Finally, thank you to our wonderful cleaner Milton Vargas Rodriguez.

3 Hearts Canvas is a London-based theatre production company dedicated to creating high-quality, socially-conscious work that pushes the boundaries of creativity within the entertainment industry.

Founded in 2019, we have produced a range of acclaimed shows, including *The Actor's Nightmare* (Park Theatre); *Smoke* (Southwark Playhouse), *SPIN* (Edinburgh Fringe – Gilded Balloon & Arcola Theatre) and C*assie & The Lights* (Southwark Playhouse & Theatre Royal Plymouth). Beyond production, we actively fundraise and manage research and development periods for bold new writing. We are passionate about championing diverse voices, treating artists with respect, paying freelancers fairly, and building creative teams that reflect the rich, dynamic communities that make the UK thrive.

## CAST

### FANTA BARRIE | Honey

Fanta Barrie graduated from Rose Bruford in 2018. Her theatre credits include *The Ministry of Lesbian Affairs* (Kiln Theatre); *The Loved Ones* (Ireland Tour); *I F*****d You In My Space Ship* (Soho Theatre); *Belly Up* (Turbine Theatre); *The Loved Ones* (Gate Theatre); *The Lovely Bones* (UK Tour); *The Amber Trap* (Theatre503) and *The Cereal Café* (The Other Place). Her television credits include *My Lady Jane*, *Mrs Sidhu Investigates*; and for film, *The Entertainer*.

### ROSS O'DONNELLAN | Christopher

Ross O'Donnellan's theatre credits include *The Beacon* (Everyman Cork); *Luck Just Kissed You Hello* (Abbey Theatre); *Julius Caesar* (Bristol Old Vic), Crave (The Wardrobe Theatre); and *Our Town* (Circomedia). His film credits include *Belfast*.

## CREATIVE

### JESSICA NORMAN | Writer

Jessica Norman is a writer for stage and screen. She's an alumnus of the Hampstead Theatre's Inspire Writers Group, Oxford Playhouse Playmakers and Soho Theatre Writers Lab.

Her other plays include: *Wilding* (long-listed for the Women's Prize for Playwriting); *The Healing* (written on attachment to the Hampstead Theatre); *The Stones and Vitriol* (Theatre 503 International Playwriting Award Longlist – developed with Oxford Playhouse).

For screen, she is developing a slate of projects including an original series with James Norton's Rabbit Track Pictures. In 2020, her short film *Embraceable You*, written and filmed during lockdown, won Best Isolation Short at the LA Motion Picture Festival.

Before becoming a writer, Jessica worked as a producer and creative associate in the West End, with development credits including *Harry Potter and the Cursed Child*.

### IMY WYATT CORNER | Director

Imy trained on the Drama Directing MA at Bristol Old Vic Theatre School.

Direction includes *The Last One* (Arcola Theatre); *The Maladies* (Kiln Theatre- Kiln Youth Theatre); *Duck* (Arcola Theatre, Jermyn St Theatre,

South East tour with Farnham Maltings); *Passing* (Park Theatre); *Scarlet Sunday* (Omnibus Theatre); *BEASTS* (Fringe First Award Winning – Zoo Playground); *A Midsummer Night's Dream* (The Grove DIY Skatepark); *Gaslight* (Playground Theatre); *Walk Swiftly & With Purpose* (Theatre503, North Wall Arts Centre); *Baby, What Blessings* (Bunker Theatre, Theatre503) and *Happy Yet?* (International Theatre, Frankfurt).

Associate direction includes *The Dance of Death* (Theatre Royal Bath & Arcola Theatre UK Tour).

Assistant direction includes *Private Lives* (Ambassador's Theatre); *Relatively Speaking* (Theatre Royal Bath UK Tour); *The Lonely Londoners* (Kiln Theatre); *Shanghai Dolls* (Kiln Theatre); *Pins & Needles* (Kiln Theatre) and *The Purists* (Kiln Theatre).

## **IZZY CARNEY** | Producer

Izzy is a theatre maker based in London. This is her debut as a producer, having worked as a director and dramaturg. Her credits include *Don't Ask Don't Get*, *Baby* (Off Comm Commended, The Space, Edinburgh Fringe 2023) and *Helium* (The Space 2023). She is passionate about new writing and stories that encourage empathy and share new perspectives. Currently working in the New Work Department at the National Theatre, Carney is also the Co-Founder of Happy Accident Theatre Company.

## **CAT FULLER** | Set and Costume Designer

Cat is a Set and Costume Designer working in Theatre and Performance. She graduated with an MA in Performance Design from Bristol Old Vic Theatre School and was a winner of The 2021 Linbury Prize.

Design credits include *The Constant Wife* (Co-Costume Design) (RSC); *Churchill in Moscow*, *Testmatch* (The Orange Tree); *Red Speedo* (Costume Design & Associate Set) (The Orange Tree); *The Maids*, *Owners* (Jermyn Street Theatre); *Scarlet Sunday* (Omnibus Theatre); *Snail* (VAULT Festival); *Flies* (Boundless Theatre & Shoreditch Town Hall); *The Sweet Science of Bruising* (The Egg, Theatre Royal Bath); *Romeo and Juliet* (Bristol Old Vic); *The Three Seagulls* (Set Design) (Bristol Old Vic); *Kyoto* (The Wardrobe Theatre); *Falling in Love Again* (Set Design) (Kings Head Theatre).

Associate design include *13 Going on 30: The Musical* (Manchester Opera House); *The Time Traveller's Wife: The Musical* (West End/Chester Storyhouse); *A Christmas Carol* (Finnish National Opera and Ballet); *Much Ado About Nothing* (National Theatre); *Home I'm Darling* (UK tour); *If You Fall* (Theatre Ad Infinitum).

Awards include: The Linbury Prize for Stage Design – 2021, The John Elvery Prize for Excellence in Stage Design – 2021, Offies nomination for Set Design of Owners at Jermyn Street Theatre.

## HUGO DODSWORTH | Light and Projection Designer

Hugo is a Performance Designer working across disciplines of set, lighting, and video design. He trained at Bristol Old Vic Theatre School after reading Italian and History of Art at UCL.

Theatre credits include *Dear Annie, I Hate You* (Pleasance Courtyard, Riverside Studios); *Dear Young Monster* (Soho Theatre, Bristol Old Vic); *Night Waking* (Mull Theatre); *Henry V, Catastrophe Bay, Babytales*, and *Loam* (Bristol Old Vic); *The Last One* (Arcola); *Mariupol* (Pleasance Courtyard, Cockpit Theatre); *Sensory Cinders* (Soho Place); *The Crucible* (the egg, Theatre Royal Bath); *Machinal, The Machinal, The White Devil, Mother Courage and her Children, Lysistrata, The Visit*, and *Between the Roots and Wings* (Royal Central School of Speech and Drama), *Angels in America, The Cherry Orchard, Balm in Gilead*, and *Darknet* (Tobacco Factory); *Answering Machines* (East Riding Theatre); *Illusion* and *Saint Joan* (Bloomsbury Theatre); *Answering Machines* (East Riding Theatre); *The Telephone* and *La Voix Humaine* (Playground Theatre); *Fame Whore* (Kings Head Theatre); *Not The End of the World* (Cockpit Theatre); *How You Died* (Old Red Lion); *The Last Days of Judas Iscariot* (The Station); *Girl in the Machine* (Wardrobe Theatre); *Romeo and Juliet* (Redgrave Theatre); *Little Light* (Tower Theatre).

## JAMIE LU | Sound Designer

Jamie is a London-based scenographer and an award-nominated sound designer.

Previous work at the Arcola includes: *Utoya, Spin, Gentlemen, The Apology, We Started to Sing, Broken Lad*.

Jamie's theatre credits as sound designer include: *English Kings Killing Foreigners, A Gig for Ghosts* (Soho Theatre); *The Poetess* (EdFringe25); *Big Big Sky, The Haunting* (New Vic Theatre); *Puppy* (King's Head); *The Society For New Cuisine, Argos Archives, George, Tiger* (Omnibus Theatre); *Still Here* (Tour and Jack Studio Theatre); *Take the Stage 2024* (Donmar Warehouse); *Autumn, Sorry We Didn't Die at Sea* (Park Theatre); *Abigail's Party* (Northern Stage and tour); *Midnight Tattoo* (Drayton Arms); *Foreverland, I'm Gonna Marry You Toby Maguire, Smoke, Tokyo Rose* (Southwark Playhouse); *The Government Inspector* (Marylebone Theatre); *Mother's Day, Grills, Declan* (Camden People's Theatre); *Ada* (National Youth Theatre); *Transit* (The Space); *Shakespeare's R&J, Hedda Gabler* (Reading Rep); *1984* (Cockpit); *Going For Gold, Road* (Chelsea Theatre); *Burnout* (R&D, Vault Festival and tour); *Iphigenia* (Hope Theatre); *fester* (Bridge House Theatre); *Paradise Lost* (Shipwright); *The Unicorn, What The Heart Wants, How To Build a Wax Figure* (Edinburgh Fringe 2022); *The Blue House* (Blue Elephant Theatre); *Dirty Hearts* (Old Red Lion Theatre). *D.O.A., A Report to an Academy, Butterfly, The Most Beautiful Woman in the World* (Baron's

Court Theatre); *Apollonia, Flowers for Algernon, Black Mary Poppins* (Focustage/Chinese Tour); *Paper Crown* (Corbett Theatre/Bloomsbury Festival); *Wild Duck* (West Side Theatre, ET Space, China); *The Sound of Music* (Chinese Tour); *Sink* (Courtyard Theatre/Edinburgh Fringe/ Southbank Centre China Changing Festival); *String* (Lion and Unicorn Theatre).

As Assistant Sound Designer: *Henry V* (Donmar Warehouse).

As Scenographer: A Thousand Papercuts Skin Dee*p* (Baron's Court Theatre); A Report to an Academy Live (online).

Sound design for Audio play: *The Dream Machine* (Fizzy Sherbet).

### HAMZA ALI | Movement Director

Hamza is a director and movement practitioner with a practice spanning direction, facilitation, and performance.

Credits include *Our Place* (Lyric Hammersmith); *The Maladies* (Kiln Theatre); *Community* (Birmingham Rep) and *Statues* (Bush Theatre). He served a Resident Director for *Kiss Marry Kill* (National Theatre Studios /Tour) and was lead performer for *Waswasa* (Birmingham Hippodrome). He has facilitated workshops for NYT, Kiln Theatre, Lung Theatre, Peut-Être, and SOLT; directed original work for The Place, Edinburgh Fringe and artsdepot; and was a visiting professional/artist at RCSSD, CSM, and University of Cambridge. Hamza holds an MA in Movement from the Royal Central School of Speech and Drama and a BA in Drama from Royal Holloway.

## CHARACTERS

**HONEY**
**CHRISTOPHER**

**NIGEL WEST**
**A GIANT PENGUIN**

The actor playing Christopher also plays Nigel West and the giant penguin.

## SETTING

A recognisable world of the here and now – and Antarctica.

## AUTHOR'S NOTES

**A note on the text**
—   is a change of timeline

,
,
,   is a fast-forward/continuation of the same timeline

( )   text in brackets can be left unsaid at your discretion

...   is a small pause, shift or beat

# ACKNOWLEDGEMENTS

Huge thanks to everyone who has supported the play's development, including all the workshop casts and creatives: John Dagleish, Gloria Obianyo, Alex Austin, Frankie Bradshaw, Matt Gavan, Bianca Stephens, Justina Kehinde, Cherelle Skeete, Ben Batt, Sean Linnen, Emily Lunnon, Brain Zeilinger, Ramin Sabi, Gareth Lake, Isabel Dixon and the Minaturists, Hannah Hauer-King, Ellie Keel and the Women's Prize for Playwriting.

Thank you to Tony Tabatznik, Diana and Allan Morgenthau and Matthew Warchus for believing in me and the production.

The Golsoncott Foundation and Arts Council England.

And The UK Antarctic Heritage Trust.

Tom Wright, who got me writing in the first place.

Johan and Ava Persson.

My writing crew including Ottilie Wilford, Jordan Waller, Sarah Power, Martha Watson-Allpress, Sid Sagar, Nancy Netherwood, Patrick Swain, Nic McQuillan, Rebecca Crookshank, Amy Powell Yeates, Alice Robb and Katy Fallon.

My brilliant agents – Florence Hyde and Grace Baxter.

Alex Kendall.

My family – Judy and Josh, Mum and Dad – for everything.

*For my grandmother Honey Summers
(who was not a Flat-Earther, for the record).*

*(Inside a crevasse in Antarctica.)*

**CHRISTOPHER.** I don't believe this...

**HONEY.** How did we...

**CHRISTOPHER.** I have to get out of here...

**HONEY.** I think you broke my fall...

**CHRISTOPHER.** I have to get out of –

Help!

**HONEY.** What are / you –

**CHRISTOPHER.** HELP!!!!

**HONEY.** There's no one up there.

**CHRISTOPHER.** PLEASE SOMEBODY HELP ME!

*(It echoes all around them.)*

**HONEY.** No one can hear you.

**CHRISTOPHER.** You're right. I'm going to die down here.

**HONEY.** You're not going / to –

**CHRISTOPHER.** Starve to death, unless hypothermia gets me first. And Charlotte, I'm never going to see Charlotte again...

**HONEY.** Stop, Christopher.

**CHRISTOPHER.** I'm never going to hold her, I'm never going to –

You...

This is your fault.

Why do bad things always happen to me?

**HONEY.** If you want to get out of here, stop, for a second and let me think.

> (**HONEY** *looks up towards the surface.*)

It must be fifteen meters...

*(Checking herself for injuries.)* I'm not even hurt...

> (**CHRISTOPHER** *starts to feel a twinge of pain in his leg.*)

Where are the ice axes and the crampons?

> (**CHRISTOPHER** *points to the surface.*)

**HONEY.** It's way too sheer to climb...

> *(She looks around them – at sheer ice, everywhere.)*

**CHRISTOPHER.** My leg, it hurts...

> (**HONEY** *hesitates, then moves closer to him. He recoils from her.*)

**HONEY.** Do you want my help or not?

> *(He lets her come closer.)*

**CHRISTOPHER.** Be careful.

**HONEY.** Keep still.

**CHRISTOPHER.** How does it look?

**HONEY.** ...

**CHRISTOPHER.** It's bad isn't it?

**HONEY.** Try putting some weight on it.

**CHRISTOPHER.** I can't...

**HONEY.** You have to try.

*(**CHRISTOPHER** slowly tries to get up, but he falls back down hard with a thud.)*

**CHRISTOPHER**. Argh!

*(The sound of cracking ice and falling snow echoes out below.)*

It really hurts.

**HONEY**. Shhh...

*(**HONEY** listens: as her eyes adjust to the darkness, she suddenly sees where they are...)*

Don't move.

**CHRISTOPHER**. What – what is it?

**HONEY**. This is a snow bridge.

**CHRISTOPHER**. What's that mean?

**HONEY**. It means this crevasse is deeper than it looks – could go on for miles below us and we don't know how thick this snow is –

**CHRISTOPHER**. Oh that's just bloody perfect, isn't it?

*(**HONEY** goes onto hands and knees and crawls towards the edge.)*

**HONEY**. I think I can see light down there...

**CHRISTOPHER**. Light?

*(She goes into her rucksack, pulls out: a length of rope.)*

**HONEY**. Yes. This is...if I can get right down to the bottom, there might be another way out.

**CHRISTOPHER**. Seems like a pretty bad idea to me.

**HONEY**. Do you have a better one?

*(**HONEY** starts to unspool the rope.)*

Up or down – that's the choice. And we've just established we can't go up.

**CHRISTOPHER.** I don't think we've explored all the – what about staying here / and.

**HONEY.** And waiting to be rescued? By – the penguins?

**CHRISTOPHER.** How do we even know the rope's long enough / to –

**HONEY.** We don't.

**CHRISTOPHER.** I'm not going down there, there's nothing you can do to make me.

**HONEY.** …

…

**CHRISTOPHER.** Honey…

**HONEY.** I'm not going to give up and die, not like this.

**CHRISTOPHER.** You can't leave me…

**HONEY.** I'm not going / to –

**CHRISTOPHER.** Try and say it with some conviction.

**HONEY.** …

**CHRISTOPHER.** Tell me the truth.

**HONEY.** My truth or yours?

**CHRISTOPHER.** Did you ever love me? Or was it all just –

I thought we –

**HONEY.** It was a story. It wasn't real.

**CHRISTOPHER.** It was, it was real.

**HONEY.** I was stupid to believe it.

…

**CHRISTOPHER**. Please...

**HONEY**. You can't walk.

**CHRISTOPHER**. I'm okay, look I'm fine I –

*(He tries to get up.)*

*(But he falls back down again, hard, in pain.)*

*(The snow bridge shakes under them.)*

**HONEY**. Careful!

**CHRISTOPHER**. We're dead anyway, so what does it matter?

You did this.

**HONEY**. No, you did. You're the one who – who –

**CHRISTOPHER**. I just wanted to believe that it was, that the world wasn't just... But it's not here. We were never going to find it.

—

*(Before.)*

*(Wetherspoons.* **HONEY** *is drinking alone. She's reading a well-thumbed book:* The Worst Journey in the World, *by Apsley Cherry-Garrard.* **CHRISTOPHER** *is standing next to her.)*

Good story?

**HONEY**. Uh... Yes.

**CHRISTOPHER**. What's it about?

**HONEY**. It's by this explorer.

**CHRISTOPHER**. Oh yeah? What did he – or she – do?

**HONEY**. I'm actually just –

**CHRISTOPHER.** Of course. Yes. I'll – sorry.

> (**CHRISTOPHER** *looks around, then goes and sits down at the next table. He sips his pint, while* **HONEY** *reads her book.*)
>
> (**HONEY** *looks over at* **CHRISTOPHER**, *who smiles at her.*)
>
> (*She goes back to her book.*)
>
> (*They sit like this for a minute.*)
>
> (**HONEY** *looks back at* **CHRISTOPHER**, *who is now pretending not to notice her.*)

**HONEY.** He went to Antarctica.

**CHRISTOPHER.** Antarctica?

**HONEY.** With Captain Scott in 1912. They did this crazy expedition to look for emperor penguin eggs out on the sea ice in the middle of the polar night. He almost died like multiple times.

**CHRISTOPHER.** What's polar night?

**HONEY.** In Antarctica, there's only one sunset and one sunrise a year. So night lasts for like six months.

**CHRISTOPHER.** How do you know that?

**HONEY.** I'm kind of obsessed.

**CHRISTOPHER.** What's your favourite thing about it?

**HONEY.** I guess, it's just so unbelievable that there's this wilderness, a whole continent at the edge of the world covered in ice, with no people.

**CHRISTOPHER.** No people sounds like heaven, sign me up.

There are penguins right?

**HONEY.** Loads of them. And – are you sure you want to –

**CHRISTOPHER.** I'm interested.

**HONEY.** Sometimes it gets so cold that the water droplets in the air freeze into ice crystals. When the sunlight hits them in a certain way, people say it looks like it's raining gold dust all around you.

**CHRISTOPHER.** Sounds magical.

**HONEY.** I'd love to see it one day.

**CHRISTOPHER.** You can't just go though, can you?

**HONEY.** It's really expensive. Me and my sister looked into it. Planned our journey and everything: first we'd catch a plane to Buenos Aires, then down to Ushuaia at the tip of Argentina, then get on a cruise ship over the Drake's Passage to the Antarctic peninsula.

**CHRISTOPHER.** How much does it cost?

**HONEY.** Ten grand at least... each.

**CHRISTOPHER.** *(Whistles.)* Well, for what it's worth, I think you'll get there one day.

**HONEY.** She won't.

**CHRISTOPHER.** ?

**HONEY.** She died.

...

**CHRISTOPHER.** Oh fucking hell, I'm so sorry.

**HONEY.** It's not your fault.

**CHRISTOPHER.** And here I was going on like a twat.

I really am / sorry.

**HONEY.** Please stop saying / sorry.

**CHRISTOPHER.** Sorry. Sorry!

**HONEY.** It's insane, she was literally the healthiest person, never got sick, only ate organic, exercised all the – everything you're supposed to do.

**CHRISTOPHER.** Cancer, was it?

**HONEY.** (Yes).

**CHRISTOPHER.** There's something wrong with the world, I tell you.

**HONEY.** It's her funeral today.

**CHRISTOPHER.** Oh.

...

**HONEY.** They played Coldplay. She fucking hated Coldplay.

**CHRISTOPHER.** What song?

**HONEY.** 'Fix You'.

**CHRISTOPHER.** No! At a –

**HONEY.** *(Half-laughing.)* I know...

She really loved it here for some reason so –

**CHRISTOPHER.** I get it – it's nice to remember her, in your own way.

Was she older or younger?

**HONEY.** Older.

**CHRISTOPHER.** Thought so.

**HONEY.** You can tell?

**CHRISTOPHER.** Not really, I'm an only child – well, sort of. I've got a half brother, much older, but we're estranged. And he is actually quite strange to be fair. Anyway –

(**CHRISTOPHER** *raises his glass.*)

To your sister.

**HONEY.** Sadie.

**CHRISTOPHER.** To Sadie.

*(HONEY raises her glass too. They cheers in the air.)*

What would you have played?

**HONEY.** I had a whole playlist, but...you really want to know?

**CHRISTOPHER.** I really do.

**HONEY.** There's this one song. We used to sing it dancing round the kitchen.

It's kind of weird.

**CHRISTOPHER.** Weird is good. Try me.

**HONEY.** I can't remember the name, but...

**CHRISTOPHER.** How does it go?

**HONEY.** Uh... Okay...

*(She hums a bit of a song. A 70s R&B, soul/reggae tune in the style of 'Too Late to Turn Back Now' by Cornelius Brothers & Sister Rose.\*)*

**CHRISTOPHER.** I love that song!

**HONEY.** Really?

**CHRISTOPHER.** *(Pretending to sing it, but clearly doesn't know it.)* Yeah! Great choice.

*(HONEY laughs.)*

**HONEY.** Did you want to come and...

---

\* A licence to produce *This Little Earth* does not include a performance licence for any third-party or copyrighted music. Licensees should create an original composition or use music in the public domain. For further information, please see the Music and Third-Party Materials Use Note on page iii.

**CHRISTOPHER.** I really don't want to impose. Get back to your book.

**HONEY.** I'd like you to.

> (**CHRISTOPHER** *gets up and sits down next to* **HONEY**.)

*(A little silence.)*

**CHRISTOPHER.** D'you believe in fate?

**HONEY.** Fate?

**CHRISTOPHER.** Sorry, I am genuinely just rubbish at small talk.

**HONEY.** What are you after here?

**CHRISTOPHER.** Honestly? Plan was: reel you in with my killer chat up lines, then win you over with my gentlemanly charms.

**HONEY.** In Wetherspoons? On the day of my sister's funeral?

**CHRISTOPHER.** Is it working?

> (**HONEY** *laughs.*)

**HONEY.** I don't believe in fate. Or anything like that. I think we're all just whirling around in the random, senseless chaos of the universe.

**CHRISTOPHER.** No way. Nothing random about it. No coincidences. Trust me.

**HONEY.** Why should I do that?

**CHRISTOPHER.** Because I wouldn't lie to you.

**HONEY.** Is that right?

**CHRISTOPHER.** Anyway, you only have to look at the state of the world, the inequality of it all, the pain, the suffering, the chaos…you really think that's all there is? Pain and chaos? It can't be.

**HONEY.** You seem very certain about things.

**CHRISTOPHER.** I'm certain about some things.

You think I'm crazy don't you?

**HONEY.** That depends – are you a born-again Christian?

**CHRISTOPHER.** God no.

**HONEY.** Far right nutter?

**CHRISTOPHER.** No!

**HONEY.** Incel?

**CHRISTOPHER.** Give me some credit! I'm a proud feminist – got a daughter so –

**HONEY.** A daughter?

**CHRISTOPHER.** Charlotte.

**HONEY.** How old is she?

**CHRISTOPHER.** Seven.

**HONEY.** (Wow).

**CHRISTOPHER.** Had her young. Me and her mum, we're not together, by the way.

**HONEY.** I'm not certain about anything, really. I'm not into politics / or –

**CHRISTOPHER.** Politicians are all a bunch of liars and truth-twisters. Can't trust them as far as you can throw them.

**HONEY.** I'll drink to that.

**CHRISTOPHER.** Do I get to know your name now?

**HONEY.** Do I get to know yours?

**CHRISTOPHER.** Christopher. Wait. Don't tell me, I'm good at this… Linda.

**HONEY.** Do I look like a Linda to you?

**CHRISTOPHER.** You're right. More of a Brenda.

**HONEY.** It's Honey.

**CHRISTOPHER.** You as sweet as your name?

**HONEY.** Here we go...

**CHRISTOPHER.** Heard that one before?

**HONEY.** Literally heard them all.

**CHRISTOPHER.** Well then I think you're sour.

**HONEY.** You're daft.

**CHRISTOPHER.** That may be, but you've got to admit it is a bit of a coincidence. Us, meeting here.

**HONEY.** It wasn't really – I mean, you came over here to talk to me.

**CHRISTOPHER.** True.

**HONEY.** Thought you didn't believe in them anyway?

**CHRISTOPHER.** Maybe I think it happened for a reason.

**HONEY.** Or maybe it's just a random bit of chance, with absolutely no meaning at all.

**CHRISTOPHER.** Or maybe...maybe it's fate.

—

*(**HONEY** and **CHRISTOPHER**, suspended by ropes, lowering themselves down through darkness into the heart of the crevasse. **CHRISTOPHER** is in pain. And it's very very slow going.)*

*(Dripping, creaking, echoing, darkness all around.)*

I don't like this... What if the rope snaps?

Are you sure you fastened it properly, what if…

**HONEY.** …

**CHRISTOPHER.** How much further?

**HONEY.** It can't be much deeper.

**CHRISTOPHER.** But it could be?

**HONEY.** Turn off your torch.

**CHRISTOPHER.** Are you joking?

**HONEY.** Turn it off, just for a second –

**CHRISTOPHER.** No!

> (**HONEY** *grabs the torch from him – there's a little tussle between them. She gets it but loses her grip on it and it falls down, away from them. After a few seconds it reaches the crevasse floor with a thud.*)
>
> (*In the darkness, a tiny, faint crack of light appears, casting a blue tinge across the ice.*)

**HONEY.** Down there. The light. Do you see it?

**CHRISTOPHER.** I …

**HONEY.** If there's light, it means there's another way out.

**CHRISTOPHER.** How do you know?

**HONEY.** I saw it in a film once.

**CHRISTOPHER.** Oh great, a film.

**HONEY.** People have survived worse than this.

**CHRISTOPHER.** I'm not an Antarctic explorer. I don't want to be here.

> (*Silence between them.*)

The worst part is, you let me fall in love with you.

**HONEY.** Don't do this now.

**CHRISTOPHER.** But I don't matter to you –

**HONEY.** You're not the victim. I know you think you are but you're not. You're the one who preyed on me, lied to / me –

**CHRISTOPHER.** Is that really what you think happened?

**HONEY.** Yes.

**CHRISTOPHER.** Why did you even want to come here?

**HONEY.** Why did you? Because you wanted to be a hero?

**CHRISTOPHER.** No.

**HONEY.** To plant your little flag and prove to everyone that –

>   (**CHRISTOPHER** *laughs.*)

Why then?

**CHRISTOPHER.** I thought it was obvious…

For you.

>   —

>   (*Before.*)

How's that for a view?

**HONEY.** Not bad.

**CHRISTOPHER.** Not bad?

**HONEY.** It's nice, yeah.

**CHRISTOPHER.** Can't believe you've never been up here.

**HONEY.** I have, just not for ages.

**CHRISTOPHER.** (*Shouts.*) WHOOOOOHOOOOO!!!!!!

**HONEY.** What are you doing?

**CHRISTOPHER.** Try it.

    WOOOHOOOO!!!!!

**HONEY.** I don't know...

**CHRISTOPHER.** Go on, it'll make you feel alive.

**HONEY.** Whoop!

**CHRISTOPHER.** ...

**HONEY.** What?

**CHRISTOPHER.** Try with some conviction.

**HONEY.** Do I have to?

**CHRISTOPHER.** No, but I will think you're a bit of a wuss if you don't.

I won't look at you, if that helps.

>*(He closes his eyes.)*

**HONEY.** You're peeking.

**CHRISTOPHER.** I'm not!

**HONEY.** ...WHOOHOOO!

**CHRISTOPHER.** How did that feel?

**HONEY.** Good, actually.

*(Louder.)* WOOOOOOOOOOOOHOOOOO!!!!

>*(She laughs.)*

>*(She sees someone below them and ducks.)*

Oh my god, it's my neighbour.

**CHRISTOPHER.** Where?

**HONEY.** Down there, with the stupid little dog.

Do you think she saw me?

**CHRISTOPHER.** I don't think she saw you. Might have heard you…

**HONEY.** Is she looking this way?

**CHRISTOPHER.** HEY, LADY!

YOUR DOG IS STUPID / AND SMALL.

**HONEY.** *(Laughing, pulling him down.)* Stop!

**CHRISTOPHER.** I say, screw her AND HER LITTLE DOG TOO.

**HONEY.** *(Laughing, pulling him back down.)* Shhh!

> (**HONEY** and **CHRISTOPHER** *on the ground together, laughing.*)

> (*A charged moment between them.*)

So you just come up here and shout at…?

**CHRISTOPHER.** Let it all out, yeah.

**HONEY.** What like once a week or?

**CHRISTOPHER.** Better than screaming into your pillow.

**HONEY.** Do you do that a lot?

**CHRISTOPHER.** Do you not?

> (**HONEY** *laughs.*)

**HONEY.** What?

**CHRISTOPHER.** You've got a really nice laugh.

**HONEY.** Oh…thank you.

…

Has she gone?

**CHRISTOPHER.** Coast is clear.

I brought some beers and some picnic bits.

**HONEY.** M&S?

**CHRISTOPHER.** You're worth it.

How about a drinking game?

**HONEY.** How old are you?

**CHRISTOPHER.** Indulge me. I'll let you pick.

**HONEY.** Alright… Two truths and a lie? Is that a drinking game?

**CHRISTOPHER.** Excellent choice. You first.

**HONEY.** I warn you, I always know when someone's lying to me, it's like a sixth sense.

**CHRISTOPHER.** I'd better make sure I never lie to you then, eh? Except for now, obviously.

**HONEY.** I'm scared of penguins. When I was little, I had a pet stick insect called Jose. And my favourite meal is a roast dinner.

**CHRISTOPHER.** You don't like roasts.

**HONEY.** Of course I like roasts! Who doesn't like roasts?

**CHRISTOPHER.** What sides though?

**HONEY.** Two kinds of potatoes: roast and mashed.

**CHRISTOPHER.** Steady on.

**HONEY.** Carrots, parsnips.

**CHRISTOPHER.** Don't forget the gravy.

**HONEY.** No gravy.

**CHRISTOPHER.** No gravy?!

**HONEY.** I don't like it.

**CHRISTOPHER.** Without gravy it's just a lump of dry meat.

**HONEY.** I don't like a wet plate.

**CHRISTOPHER.** You're an animal.

**HONEY.** Which was the lie?

**CHRISTOPHER.** The stick insect.

**HONEY.** ...

**CHRISTOPHER.** Penguins?? How can you be scared of penguins?

**HONEY.** Scared is maybe the wrong word, more like trepidatious. They're way more intelligent than anyone gives them credit. I think they deserve our respect and maybe, a little, our fear. Anyway Christopher, I believe I just won that round, so it's your turn to drink.

**CHRISTOPHER.** You're gonna get me drunk!

**HONEY.** That's the plan.

**CHRISTOPHER.** To take advantage of me?

**HONEY.** Maybe a little.

*(A charged beat.)*

Your turn.

**CHRISTOPHER.** You ready?

I make an excellent roast dinner, like MasterChef excellent.

**HONEY.** Are you flexing, Christopher?

**CHRISTOPHER.** *(Laughs.)* I love…swimming. And… I once had a beer with Ian Beale off of EastEnders.

**HONEY.** I don't think you love swimming. In fact, I don't think you can swim at all.

**CHRISTOPHER.** I can swim, I just never got taught so it's more of a doggy paddle.

**HONEY.** Which one's Ian Beale?

**CHRISTOPHER.** He was married to Sharon? Had a feud with Phil Mitchell?

It was pretty huge.

*(A little silence as they drink.)*

I have to say you are weirdly good / at –

**HONEY.** Told you. Sixth sense.

**CHRISTOPHER.** Do you ever get the feeling that…

Actually d'you know what? Don't worry about it.

**HONEY.** What?

**CHRISTOPHER.** It probably sounds…

**HONEY.** Go on.

**CHRISTOPHER.** I just wondered if you ever feel like that but on a bigger scale. Like…we're all being lied to?

**HONEY.** It does feel like something is deeply wrong with the world, if that's what you mean?

**CHRISTOPHER.** That's how I feel.

I actually think there's a lot They're not telling us.

**HONEY.** Who?

**CHRISTOPHER.** The people in charge.

**HONEY.** Like what?

**CHRISTOPHER.** It's just the way the world's set up isn't it? For example: you think it's a coincidence that half the world is poor? That black and brown people are systematically disenfranchised and oppressed? Course not. It's because it suits some people to keep it that way. One rule for 'Them' and another rule for everyone else.

**HONEY.** It's fucked up, but it's always been like that – a few people profiting from everyone else's misery.

**CHRISTOPHER.** This is gonna sound…

**HONEY.** …

**CHRISTOPHER.** Sometimes, it feels like They're telling me the sky is pink, but I know it's blue cos I can fucking see it.

**HONEY.** It is blue.

**CHRISTOPHER.** Exactly, that's what I'm saying.

Do you want to know what Charlotte's first word was? 'Why'. Children are so wise. They know to question things, not to accept the reality that's presented to us. And I don't think we should just accept it, the way things are.

**HONEY.** She sounds clever.

**CHRISTOPHER.** She's a tiny prodigy. And I know every dad probably says his little girl's a genius, but with her it's actually true.

**HONEY.** My dad never said that.

**CHRISTOPHER.** He was wrong because you're clearly extremely intelligent.

**HONEY.** Oh yeah?

**CHRISTOPHER.** Yeah. You question things.

> (**CHRISTOPHER** *and* **HONEY** *are close to each other now.*)

There's this YouTuber – a guy called Nigel West. I've been following him for a while. Sometimes I think he's the only one who talks any sense. He does these videos, proves all the ways They've been hiding the truth from us, keeping us in the dark. Nigel says we have a choice: to see the world as it really is and if we choose to see it…we have the power to change everything.

**HONEY.** Big words.

**CHRISTOPHER.** See that's the lie They're selling us: that we're not powerful.

**HONEY.** Sounds kind of like – red pill, blue pill...

**CHRISTOPHER.** Which would you choose?

**HONEY.** I don't know... I don't feel powerful.

**CHRISTOPHER.** I think you are.

> *(We think they might kiss but...)*

Can I show you something?

—

> *(**HONEY** and **CHRISTOPHER** have just reached the bottom of the crevasse.)*

> *(**HONEY** looks around and finds the torch they dropped. Switches it on and it stutters to life.)*

**HONEY.** Still works!

This place is huge... There are crevasses that are the size of St. Paul's Cathedral, bigger even.

**CHRISTOPHER.** I don't want to think about that.

**HONEY.** It's actually kind of beautiful. Some of this ice is probably millions of years old...

**CHRISTOPHER.** Is it just me or is it colder down here?

> *(**HONEY** shines the torch at the walls around them.)*

What are you doing?

**HONEY.** Looking for a way out.

> *(She shines it in one direction.)*

> *(No joy. She tries another.)*

*(Then another.)*

*(Just ice on all sides.)*

*(She turns the torch off.)*

*(The blue light is high up, faint and distant.)*

That's not possible...

**CHRISTOPHER.** We're trapped down here, aren't we?

**HONEY.** ...

(**HONEY** *turns the torch back on. Checks what supplies they have.*)

You've got the burner right? I've got a canister of gas and a few biscuits and butter, some water. If we ration what we have, we can wait a few days for your leg to heal and then –

**CHRISTOPHER.** Then what?

**HONEY.** Then, maybe the ice / will –

**CHRISTOPHER.** Will magically melt?

**HONEY.** Ice moves, constantly, it's not static.

**CHRISTOPHER.** I told you this was a bad – We should've stayed where we were / and.

**HONEY.** And waited for the snow bridge to melt underneath us?

**CHRISTOPHER.** At least we could still see the sky up there.

*(Silence.)*

I should never have trusted you.

**HONEY.** That makes two of us.

**CHRISTOPHER.** I'm cold.

**HONEY.** I'll make us a cup of tea.

> *(She gets out their burner stove: tries to turn it on, but it burns out immediately.)*

No, no, come on...

> *(She tries again – it burns out again.)*

Shit...

> *(She tries again – it happens again.)*

SHIT.

> *(It echoes around them. The faint sounds of ice cracking.)*

At least try and help.

**CHRISTOPHER.** What's the point?

**HONEY.** So we don't die a slow and painful death?

**CHRISTOPHER.** Too late for that.

**HONEY.** Just try and fix it!

Can you?

**CHRISTOPHER.** Not without parts.

**HONEY.** Stupid piece of –

...

It's going to be okay. We've still got some water left in the flask. We'll give it twenty-four hours and / then –

**CHRISTOPHER.** How is any of this ever going to be okay?

**HONEY.** I know it doesn't look good / but –

**CHRISTOPHER.** Doesn't look good? Doesn't look good?!

> *(**CHRISTOPHER** starts to laugh. A chuckle at first, then it turns into full belly laughter.)*

**HONEY.** Stop it. It's not –

> *(He's hysterical now.)*

It's not funny!

**CHRISTOPHER.** I know it's not funny.

> *(Suddenly he stops laughing.)*

This place is a nightmare.

—

> *(Before. Christopher's basement. There is a big object in the centre of the room, covered in a sheet.)*

> *(**HONEY** and **CHRISTOPHER** have just slept together.)*

**HONEY.** Quite the man cave you've got down here.

**CHRISTOPHER.** 'Scuse the mess.

**HONEY.** You fixed all of this stuff?

**CHRISTOPHER.** Always been pretty handy. When I was younger, I used to take everything apart, wanted to know how it all worked. Mum used to come home, find her hairdryer in bits.

**HONEY.** Bet she loved that.

**CHRISTOPHER.** I spent years doing the rat race. Suit and tie and taking the train into work at dawn...and I remember, there was this one morning, I was coming out of Waterloo station and I was standing on the zebra crossing and there was all these people, all these grey-looking people, coming towards me the other way, in their suits just like mine and... I can't explain it. It was like I just woke up. Quit my job that very day and, honestly? It was best decision I ever made. I love working for myself, working with my hands –

**HONEY.** Sounds nice.

**CHRISTOPHER.** You're a fixer too!

**HONEY.** IT support?

**CHRISTOPHER.** It's interesting.

**HONEY.** The one thing it is not is interesting. I'm just sat in this grey little booth for eight hours a day, can't even see out the window. And the people...the people make me want to gauge my eyes out with a rusty spoon.

**CHRISTOPHER.** They'll be replacing you all with robots soon, anyway, won't they?

**HONEY.** Not soon enough.

Is this...

**CHRISTOPHER.** (Yes)

**HONEY.** She looks like you.

**CHRISTOPHER.** Do you want kids or?

**HONEY.** Bit early for that question isn't it?

**CHRISTOPHER.** I didn't mean...

**HONEY.** Teasing, sorry... I can't have them.

**CHRISTOPHER.** Oh.

**HONEY.** This doctor messed me up good and proper when I was younger so –

**CHRISTOPHER.** Honey that's... I'm so sorry.

**HONEY.** Probably for the best. The women in my family don't exactly have the maternal gene.

**CHRISTOPHER.** I'm sure you would've – But kids break your heart, trust me.

...

**HONEY.** What are you doing over there?

**CHRISTOPHER.** Are you ready for me to change your life?

**HONEY.** I think so?

**CHRISTOPHER.** Are you sure? It's quite like, big.

**HONEY.** Okay…

**CHRISTOPHER.** And you can't go back once you know.

**HONEY.** I'm sure!

**CHRISTOPHER.** You have to promise not to laugh.

**HONEY.** Why would I laugh?

**CHRISTOPHER.** I've not shown this to anyone else, so just promise me you won't.

**HONEY.** I promise.

**CHRISTOPHER.** Maybe it's a bad idea.

**HONEY.** How bad can it be?

**CHRISTOPHER.** It's not bad. It's amazing it's just…okay.

That feeling you described. The feeling that something is deeply wrong with the world. You're right to feel that way, because it's true. Something really is wrong.

(**CHRISTOPHER** *hesitates.*)

(*Then he pulls the cover off the object in the centre of the room.* **HONEY** *looks at it for a moment.*)

Ta dah!

…

Say something.

**HONEY.** What am I looking at?

**CHRISTOPHER.** It's a model of the Earth. See you've got the continents here: the Americas, Africa, Europe, Asia… And then Antarctica goes all the way around.

**HONEY.** All the way around?

**CHRISTOPHER.** That's why I wanted to show it to you. This is what the people in charge are hiding from us. Their biggest secret. The thing 'They' don't want you to know.

**HONEY.** …

**CHRISTOPHER.** The True Earth.

**HONEY.** But it's…

**CHRISTOPHER.** Yes. It is. It's… (Flat).

>   …
>
>   (**HONEY** *laughs.*)

You promised not to / laugh.

**HONEY.** This is a joke. You're joking –

**CHRISTOPHER.** Course I'm not/ joking.

**HONEY.** You don't actually believe –

**CHRISTOPHER.** I shouldn't have brought you here.

**HONEY.** It's very detailed. What's it made of?

**CHRISTOPHER.** Wood, mostly. Bit of papier-mâché for the texture.

**HONEY.** What's that, there?

**CHRISTOPHER.** That's the Edge of the World. And next to it, here, is the giant ice wall that keeps all the water in and stops us falling off.

**HONEY.** The giant ice wall?

**CHRISTOPHER.** You're skeptical I get it. But it's like *The Truman Show*.

**HONEY**. The film?

**CHRISTOPHER**. Practically a documentary. Christof, remember, he's the Creator in it. He says we all just accept the reality we're presented with, but we shouldn't because 'They' are lying to us, controlling what we see.

**HONEY**. The government are?

**CHRISTOPHER**. They're just the puppets. There are people behind them, pulling the strings.

**HONEY**. Why would anyone do that?

**CHRISTOPHER**. To keep us oppressed while 'They' stay powerful and rich. It's better for 'Them' if we feel insignificant and small: just a tiny spec of dust on a planet orbiting a sun in one of an infinite number of solar systems. Because if we knew how powerful we really were…

**HONEY**. ?

**CHRISTOPHER**. If more people knew, it'd be the end of society as we know it.

**HONEY**. What about space?

**CHRISTOPHER**. It's fake. A simulation.

**HONEY**. What about the moon landings, all of that.

**CHRISTOPHER**. A massive hoax.

**HONEY**. It's on film, you can literally watch / it.

**CHRISTOPHER**. I'm not saying there's no skill involved. There's artistry to creating the world.

**HONEY**. But this is –

**CHRISTOPHER**. ?

**HONEY**. This is…conspiracy theory, isn't it?

**CHRISTOPHER**. They call them 'conspiracy theories' to silence us. They're not theories, this is all based in real measurements, in research, in facts. Also – I don't understand why 'conspiracy' is such a dirty word. Think about all the conspiracies that turned out to be true! The Tuskegee Medical trials, look those up... Erin Brockevitch, they tried to stop her investigating but she was right, the water was – and Iraq and weapons of mass destruction and the Catholic Church abusing children and Jeffrey Epstein's secret paedophile ring and and Covid! Coming from a secret Chinese Lab, that was a 'conspiracy theory', until suddenly it wasn't and when you think about how rich the elites got off of that one, I know it goes much deeper / than –

**HONEY.** But how do you get from that / to –

**CHRISTOPHER.** You said it yourself. The world is wrong, things are upside down. Doctors destroying health, governments destroying freedom, the mainstream media destroying information... All of these things, they aren't just isolated events. It's a whole system that's rigged against us. And it takes people like me, brave people who question things, to get to the truth.

I know it's a lot. I'm not asking you to believe it right now. All I'm asking is that you try to understand.

**HONEY.** I'm sorry but –

**CHRISTOPHER.** Can I show you a video? One of Nigel West's. He puts it way way better than I can.

**HONEY.** I can't do this.

**CHRISTOPHER.** Do you think I want to believe this stuff? I wish I didn't, but once you see it, the lies, the deception, you can't un-see it.

**HONEY.** I have to go.

**CHRISTOPHER.** Charlotte's mum left me because I believed all this. She won't let me see my daughter. I've got no rights, I'm her dad, but just cos we weren't married I can never see my own daughter again. Tell me, how that's fair?

**HONEY.** It's not, the world isn't fair, but it doesn't mean that any of this / is –

**CHRISTOPHER.** I know it seems crazy, I felt like that at first, but just give it a chance. One video and if you hate it you'll never have to speak to me or see me ever again.

**HONEY.** It seems crazy because it – because you are completely fucking crazy Christopher.

**CHRISTOPHER.** I'm not –

**HONEY.** Don't contact me.

**CHRISTOPHER.** This doesn't have to – we can believe different things, can't we?

*(But she's already gone.)*

—

*(The crevasse.)*

*(**HONEY** is alone.)*

*(And for a moment, the crevasse blends into another space. **HONEY**, lit by the glow of a screen, her eyes fixed as flickering images dance across her face.)*

*(The images flash, speed up…until we suddenly snap back to:)*

*(Darkness.)*

*(Creaking, dripping ice.)*

*(The blue light glows above them, tantalising, in the distance.)*

*(**HONEY** and **CHRISTOPHER** sitting huddled on separate sides, trying to get warm.)*

> (**CHRISTOPHER** *groans in pain.*)

**HONEY.** Can I touch you?

**CHRISTOPHER.** …

**HONEY.** We need the warmth. Sharing our body heat is the only thing that will help.

**CHRISTOPHER.** See that? It's the dividing line. Don't come any closer.

**HONEY.** You're acting like a child.

> (*Silence.*)

I'm thirsty.

How much water do we have left?

> (**CHRISTOPHER** *opens the flask, takes a swig.*)

Give it here.

> (*He goes to pass it to her, but starts to empty it onto the ice.*)

What are you doing?

Stop it!

> (*She goes to wrestle the flask out of his hands.*)

You know we can't melt any more ice.

**CHRISTOPHER.** What do you think will kill us first – hypothermia or dehydration? Shall we take a little bet?

> (**HONEY** *grabs the flask from* **CHRISTOPHER**. *She looks inside, tries to take a drink. It's empty.*)

**HONEY.** Why did you do that?

**CHRISTOPHER.** Why does anyone do anything?

**HONEY.** Do you think I want to be down here either? Do you think I want to die?

**CHRISTOPHER.** I don't know anything about you.

**HONEY.** I think you liked it. Being in control –

**CHRISTOPHER.** No –

**HONEY.** Pulling the strings –

**CHRISTOPHER.** NO!

**HONEY.** You need to stop blaming other people for everything, start taking responsibility / for –

**CHRISTOPHER.** You're the reason we're down here. You're the one who needs to take responsibility for –

*(A wave of pain: he clasps his leg in agony.)*

You pushed me off a crevasse, Honey.

**HONEY.** And you pulled me over the edge with you.

—

*(Before.)*

I wasn't sure which house was yours, I've gone up and down the street knocking, tried those flats on the corner, even though I knew you didn't live in a – and then I had this horrible feeling like maybe I was wrong and this wasn't your road at all and that I'd walk up and down forever and never find you.

How have you been?

**CHRISTOPHER.** …

**HONEY.** Stupid question. I've not been great, to be honest, if that makes you feel any – I stopped going to work. Stopped going anywhere, really. It's weird, I realised without Sadie there's actually no one who cares what I do, like whether I live or die. *(Laughs.)*

I've been thinking about you a lot, is the truth. I was going to call but I thought maybe you wouldn't… And so I'm here to tell you that I'm sorry. I feel really really bad for what I said and for leaving like I did and –

**CHRISTOPHER.** I thought you never wanted to see me again?

**HONEY.** I'm really sorry I made you feel like that.

**CHRISTOPHER.** Alright, you've said that now so.

**HONEY.** I've been online a lot. And um…it's weird, I was scrolling and one of Nigel West's reels came up. And I watched one. I say one – I watched a lot of them actually.

**CHRISTOPHER.** If you're here to laugh at me again then –

**HONEY.** I'm not. It was like the more I watched, the more stuff came up: podcasts, images, more videos…and he is a really smart guy and he does make sense of a lot of – It's like you said, when you think about everything. They're already lying to us about. All the medical stuff and Covid, like, I knew that was a Lab Leak right from the start, and everyone looked at me funny for saying that and 'They' covered that up didn't they? So what else have 'They' – anyway, I wanted to show you…

*(She gets out her copy of* The Worst Journey in the World.*)*

I was reading this again and it's so weird, Cherry talks about… Where is it? Sorry, I know it's here… Yes, look he talks about an ice cliff, running for hundreds of miles to the East!

A giant ice cliff! In Antarctica! And I thought that can't be right, it's too big of a coincidence, so I looked in Captain Scott's diaries to cross-reference and he keeps talking about something called: 'The Great Barrier'. And then, this is the weirdest thing, no-one ever mentions it again. I literally can't find it anywhere.

**CHRISTOPHER.** ...

**HONEY.** The Great Barrier! What if it's the Ice Wall from your model?

**CHRISTOPHER.** Ha. Ha. Ha.

**HONEY.** I really think this might be evidence / of –

**CHRISTOPHER.** Actually you know what, just fuck off cos I've got things to do.

**HONEY.** I'm being serious. I thought we could investigate this, you know, together.

...

**CHRISTOPHER.** I want you to go.

**HONEY.** Sorry. Yeah. Okay.

*(**HONEY** goes to leave but then:)*

I didn't tell you, but Sadie was – After she got ill, she got sent this post. She started to believe that the doctors were hiding the real cures from her. Wouldn't have any of the treatment they wanted her to have…. I didn't – I couldn't understand…. But, I don't know, maybe there's something in all this after all.

*(A little pause.)*

*(**CHRISTOPHER** takes the book from her.)*

**CHRISTOPHER.** Is this your annotation or –

**HONEY.** It's Sadie's. This is her copy. And there, look.

I think she wanted me to find it.

**CHRISTOPHER.** ...

**HONEY.** So?

**CHRISTOPHER.** So you're right, it is weird.

**HONEY.** Isn't it?

I really need you to forgive me.

**CHRISTOPHER.** I don't know Honey… after Louise, my ex – after she left me, I kind of made this promise to myself that I would never let anyone treat me like that again –

**HONEY.** You're right. It's fine, I get it.

> (**HONEY** *turns to go.*)

**CHRISTOPHER.** But –

You really mean what you –

**HONEY.** I do.

**CHRISTOPHER.** Then… (alright)

**HONEY.** Really? Are you sure?

**CHRISTOPHER.** Careful or I might change my mind.

**HONEY.** Thank you.

> (*She hugs him.*)

> (*They hold each other for a moment, which lingers.*)

> (**HONEY** *pulls away.*)

And I thought we could go.

**CHRISTOPHER.** Go where?

**HONEY.** …

**CHRISTOPHER.** Antarctica?!

**HONEY.** Hear me out.

**CHRISTOPHER.** I'm sorry but you've seriously lost the plot now.

**HONEY.** I know it's mad but –

**CHRISTOPHER.** We can't just go to Antarctica.

**HONEY.** Why not?

**CHRISTOPHER.** Because you can't just go to –

**HONEY.** If it's there, I want to see it for myself: the ice wall at the edge of the world! We could take cameras and document it properly and prove to people that it's / actually –

**CHRISTOPHER.** I don't know why we're even talking about this.

**HONEY.** I've never done anything meaningful in my life before, I've never had a purpose or really wanted anything and something about this, about you… I can't explain it I just, I have to do it, I have to go.

What are you afraid of?

**CHRISTOPHER.** I'm not afraid.

**HONEY.** "The truth can withstand investigation", isn't that what Nigel West says?

**CHRISTOPHER.** I thought you said it was expensive.

**HONEY.** I just got Sadie's life insurance through. I'll pay for our plane tickets to Argentina and the cruise ship. That'll get us as far as the peninsula. Then all we'll need to do is steal a Zodiac boat from the ship / and –

**CHRISTOPHER.** You know how crazy you sound right now?

**HONEY.** Isn't it worth a shot?

**CHRISTOPHER.** We'd never make it.

**HONEY.** I think we will.

**CHRISTOPHER.** And what about when we get to Antarctica, if we get there, what will we do then? Did you think about that?

**HONEY.** We'll explore, we'll find the edge –

**CHRISTOPHER.** One problem: I'm not an explorer and neither are you.

**HONEY.** We just need to do a bit of training, it's not that hard.

**CHRISTOPHER.** We barely know each other, this is –

**HONEY.** I feel like I've known you forever. It's like you said: we met for a reason. This is the reason Christopher. But if you don't feel the same way –

**CHRISTOPHER.** No. I do. I just –

...

We'd have to leave everything behind.

**HONEY.** I've got nothing to stay for. Sadie's gone. I don't speak to Mum.

**CHRISTOPHER.** I've got a daughter.

**HONEY.** We're going to come back. And just imagine if we went there and came back with proof!

**CHRISTOPHER.** I don't need proof. I know what's there.

**HONEY.** Not for you, for everyone else. Show them you're not… Maybe she'd even let you see Charlotte again.

Also I've bought them already. The tickets so –

**CHRISTOPHER.** You're really serious about this?

**HONEY.** (Yes)

**CHRISTOPHER.** This is – you are –

**HONEY.** Crazy, I know. But this is also the first time in a long while that I actually feel alive. You make me feel like that…like I'm awake for the first time.

*(**CHRISTOPHER** looks at **HONEY** and laughs.)*

**HONEY.** What? What is it?

**CHRISTOPHER.** Okay.

**HONEY.** Okay, like…okay yes?

**CHRISTOPHER.** Okay, yes.

>  (**HONEY** *laughs.*)

**HONEY.** I can't believe it.

**CHRISTOPHER.** We're actually going to…

> *(They laugh.)*

> *(It echoes all around…)*

> —

> *(**HONEY** and **CHRISTOPHER** in the crevasse.)*

> *(The rumble of ice all around them. It's moving, it's alive.)*

**HONEY.** Are you awake?

**CHRISTOPHER.** Mmmm.

**HONEY.** We have to stay awake…

**CHRISTOPHER.** Shhhh…

**HONEY.** There must be something here we can eat…

> *(**HONEY** gets out objects from her bag but everything is frozen solid.)*

I'm so hungry…

> *(The torch suddenly judders and goes out.)*

No, no…

*(She hits the torch, but it's stopped working completely.)*

No!

*(In the darkness, we might notice that the blue light from earlier has got, ever so slightly brighter.)*

*(And that there is someone – or something – else in the crevasse, with them.)*

*(A dark shadow.)*

*(**HONEY** lights a match.)*

*(It goes out.)*

—

*(Before.)*

It's not everything, but it's a start. Proper winter coats, thick socks, thermals – merino wool look. It's what they took to Antarctica in Scott and Cherry's day, and it's still the best money can buy.

**CHRISTOPHER**. I'll pay you back.

**HONEY**. It's alright.

**CHRISTOPHER**. I want to.

**HONEY**. The cold will be our main enemy out there.

**CHRISTOPHER**. How cold does it get?

**HONEY**. Minus twenty at the warmest.

**CHRISTOPHER**. Sunglasses?

**HONEY**. For the snow blindness. It's bright bright white everywhere and twenty-four-hour daylight. One sunset and one sunrise a year.

**CHRISTOPHER.** How do I look?

**HONEY.** Routine and structure, they're literally everything. We'll go in four-hour cycles. Four hours of travelling then we'll eat, then sleep for four hours, then we'll get up and start it all again.

**CHRISTOPHER.** Here's the burner.

**HONEY.** This'll be our lifeline. We'll use it to melt snow for drinking water and defrost our food. I brought a compass, but it'll probably stop working when we get there, Nigel West says 'They' have this electromagnetic forcefield out at the NASA base in Florida, use currents to scramble the magnetic waves the closer you get to the wall. He talks about it in his book.

**CHRISTOPHER.** *What on Earth*?

**HONEY.** His memoir – *Living on The Edge*.

**CHRISTOPHER.** A classic.

**HONEY.** I've sent him a DM, by the way.

**CHRISTOPHER.** You sent a DM to Nigel West?

**HONEY.** Told him what we were planning.

**CHRISTOPHER.** Has he replied?

**HONEY.** Not yet but –

**CHRISTOPHER.** You're full of surprises.

**HONEY.** I thought he could be useful. Maybe he'll share our footage on his channels when we get back.

**CHRISTOPHER.** Two cameras?

**HONEY.** One to film the edge of the world when we find it and another for you to film me filming it – otherwise people will just say it's not real, that it's a green screen or a studio or whatever. We can't bring phones with us, obviously, it'd be way too easy for 'Them' to track us.

**CHRISTOPHER**. You've thought of everything, haven't you? ... Hey – you got anything to protect us against the penguins?

**HONEY**. Very funny.

**CHRISTOPHER**. What about the polar bears?

**HONEY**. There aren't any in Antarctica.

**CHRISTOPHER**. They don't exist, anyway. They're just normal bears painted white. They put them in the pictures to scare us away.

**HONEY**. You're daft.

**CHRISTOPHER**. What are these little plastic bags for?

**HONEY**. ...

**CHRISTOPHER**. No...

**HONEY**. We can't leave any trace of ourselves behind.

**CHRISTOPHER**. I draw the line at shitting in a plastic bag.

**HONEY**. It's easy, don't worry, it'll freeze as soon as it comes out, so you literally can't miss.

**CHRISTOPHER**. I'm not even going to ask how you know that.

**HONEY**. ...

**CHRISTOPHER**. Everything alright?

**HONEY**. Seeing all this stuff, makes it feel real...

**CHRISTOPHER**. This was your idea...

**HONEY**. Do you think I'm mental?

**CHRISTOPHER**. Yes. But I also think you're fearless.

**HONEY**. Thank you. For –

**CHRISTOPHER**. I couldn't let you go alone.

**HONEY**. I mean it.

**CHRISTOPHER.** I'd follow you anywhere.

**HONEY.** Even to the ends of the earth?

**CHRISTOPHER.** Especially to the ends of the earth.

**HONEY.** So what do you think? Are you ready for this?

**CHRISTOPHER.** Ready as I'll ever be.

,

,

,

*(The deck of a cruise ship, heading to Antarctica.)*

**HONEY.** In my defence, it's the Drake's Passage. Like, infamously the roughest sea on earth.

**CHRISTOPHER.** Don't worry about it.

**HONEY.** It's embarrassing. You shouldn't've had to / see –

**CHRISTOPHER.** I can't un-see it, either. You, projectile vomiting across / the –

**HONEY.** *(Laughing.)* Shut up!

**CHRISTOPHER.** You still look beautiful. Even when you're retching.

**HONEY.** Is that supposed to be a compliment?

**CHRISTOPHER.** Do you think you'll manage dinner?

**HONEY.** You've got a stomach of steel.

**CHRISTOPHER.** It was just me in the dining room last night. Ate an entire roast chicken all on my / own.

**HONEY.** Please don't talk to me about roast chicken…

You're like Sadie. She never got sick. I was the sickly one, always throwing up.

*(They look out to sea.)*

**CHRISTOPHER.** Pretty magnificent, eh?

**HONEY.** We'll hit the peninsula tomorrow. So, I was thinking we should steal the Zodiac boat in the morning, early, before anyone can cotton on. We're not far from land now, it shouldn't take us long / to –

**CHRISTOPHER.** Tomorrow?

**HONEY.** ?

**CHRISTOPHER.** It just feels soon…

**HONEY.** I told you not to get too comfortable with the nice beds and the buffets.

**CHRISTOPHER.** We could stay one more night.

**HONEY.** It's not a holiday. And the longer we stay, the more risk / that.

**CHRISTOPHER.** Tomorrow then.

What was that?

**HONEY.** What?

**CHRISTOPHER.** There's another, there – look!

**HONEY.** Whales! Humpbacks I think…

**CHRISTOPHER.** Oh my goodness…

**HONEY.** They're –

**CHRISTOPHER.** Huge…

It's swimming under the – is that safe?

**HONEY.** Are you freaked out right now?

**CHRISTOPHER.** No…

**HONEY.** They're not going to hurt us, they're gentle.

It looks like they're dancing…

*(They watch the whales for a moment.* **CHRISTOPHER** *looks at* **HONEY**.*)*

**CHRISTOPHER.** You're just like her.

**HONEY.** ?

**CHRISTOPHER.** Charlotte. You reminded me of her, just then.

**HONEY.** I reminded you of your daughter?

**CHRISTOPHER.** Sorry is that a weird thing to – I just mean…she would absolutely love this too.

She had one of those little plastic whales for bath time that squirted water out. Always wanted me there. Said I did it better than her mum. But that was… she's probably grown out of it now.

**HONEY.** Sounds like you were good at it, being her dad.

**CHRISTOPHER.** No-one teaches you, but nothing really made sense in my life before… don't get me wrong, it was absolutely terrifying. I'd watch her sleeping at night, check in on her every few minutes just to see if she was still breathing and I'd see her little eyes flickering under their lids, dreaming about beautiful things, and I'd have these thoughts… about war and famine and murder and pain… and just to look at this tiny perfect child that is completely innocent of all that, completely dependent on me, knowing that I can't save her from all the terrible things there are in this world, it was –

**HONEY.** I'm sorry, about all of it.

**CHRISTOPHER.** I'm sorry too.

…

**HONEY.** With Sadie… it just feels so unreal that she gone. Like she's left this physical gaping hole in the world that only I can see.

**CHRISTOPHER**. You know you can talk to me about her.

**HONEY**. I want to. I want to be able to think about all the – but all I can remember is the last time –

She was in so much pain. You could see it by then... Growing through her breast, out of her body...

**CHRISTOPHER**. That's...horrible.

**HONEY**. I was angry at her. I wanted to convince her to, force her to –

**CHRISTOPHER**. She sounds brave. It takes a lot to stick to what you believe, in the face of everything.

**HONEY**. She was, really brave. I can see that now. And stubborn. *(Half-laughs.)* Always knew better about everything. Always telling me what to do, ever since she could talk.

...

What do you think happens to us after?

**CHRISTOPHER**. I don't know.

I think it's probably like sleep.

**HONEY**. People say that to make you feel better, but what if it's just more pain?

**CHRISTOPHER**. Whatever it is, it's rubbish.

**HONEY**. Dying? *(Laughs.)* Yeah, it's rubbish.

**CHRISTOPHER**. I know it's different, but with Charlotte, it was all so out of my – I spent a lot of time after trying to forget that she ever – Didn't want to talk about her, or think about her. I felt so guilty but...none of it is your fault.

**HONEY**. ...

**CHRISTOPHER**. Life hurts.

**HONEY**. I know.

**CHRISTOPHER**. I know you do.

(**CHRISTOPHER** *puts out his hand.*)

**HONEY**. What are you...?

**CHRISTOPHER**. You said they're dancing.

**HONEY**. So?

**CHRISTOPHER**. So we can't let them dance alone.

**HONEY**. What if someone sees us?

**CHRISTOPHER**. Humour me.

**HONEY**. There's no music.

(*The sound of the whales is joined by other sounds: the sounds of Antarctica, of water lapping and rushing, of cracking and moving ice.*)

(**CHRISTOPHER** *takes* **HONEY**'s *hand.*)

I love you.

**CHRISTOPHER**. You...

**HONEY**. Is that too soon, or –

**CHRISTOPHER**. I love you too.

**HONEY**. You do?

**CHRISTOPHER**. I've loved you ever since the first moment we met. It's like I look at you and I can see our whole lives laid out together.

**HONEY**. You're so certain...

**CHRISTOPHER**. About you.

**HONEY**. I feel like you know all of me.

(*They dance together.*)

*(They kiss.)*

*(It turns into something else: something deep and urgent.)*

*(The whales dance around them.)*

*(Blue and white icebergs rise up all around.)*

,

,

,

*(Bright polar sunlight.)*

**CHRISTOPHER.** Antarctica!

*(**HONEY** drinks it in.)*

Well…say something.

**HONEY.** …

**CHRISTOPHER.** You're not disappointed, are you?

**HONEY.** Disappointed? No. There aren't any words…

**CHRISTOPHER.** Look at those icebergs, they're –

**HONEY.** I've never seen anything so – and its not white here, I thought it would all be white but it's not it's blue and purple and gold! People say when you get here, it's like arriving on a whole different planet… I know what they mean now. I don't think I'll ever forget this moment, as long as I live.

**CHRISTOPHER.** Thought you said it would be cold?

**HONEY.** It's warmer than I expected but it'll get colder inland. The closer we get to the edge.

**CHRISTOPHER.** And I thought there to be more here if I'm honest, more trees or –

**HONEY.** There are no trees in Antarctica. Although the craziest thing, all this used to be a rainforest.

**CHRISTOPHER.** Now you're having me on.

**HONEY.** It's true. Hundreds of millions of years ago, it was hot and there were dinosaurs.

**CHRISTOPHER.** What's that smell?

**HONEY.** Penguins… a whole colony…

**CHRISTOPHER.** You've gotta admit, they are kind of cute.

**HONEY.** Don't look at them!

**CHRISTOPHER.** Why not?

**HONEY.** If you give them eye contact, they'll come over!

*(***CHRISTOPHER** *laughs.)*

*(Then.)*

*(A rumble from somewhere.)*

**CHRISTOPHER.** What was that?

**HONEY.** The ice. Terrain here's changing all the time.

**CHRISTOPHER.** Changing?

**HONEY.** Moving. Ice doesn't stay still, it's alive…

*(***CHRISTOPHER** *inspects the ice under his feet, suspiciously.)*

You got everything from the boat?

**CHRISTOPHER.** All present and correct.

**HONEY.** We should start filming now. We need to document everything: the whole journey from here, to the edge.

*(**CHRISTOPHER** is looking through their stuff.)*

I really think we're going to make it, don't you?

**CHRISTOPHER.** …

**HONEY.** Christopher?

**CHRISTOPHER.** Huh? Yeah –

**HONEY.** What do you think's on the other side of the edge?

Did you watch that crazy Nigel West video where he says there's evidence that if you go off the world on one side you emerge on the other, like a Pac-Man –

**CHRISTOPHER.** They're not here. The cameras they're – They must be here…

**HONEY.** I asked you before / we –

**CHRISTOPHER.** I definitely put them in the Zodiac, I know I did. I remember seeing them. They were on the deck and I put them in, I –

**HONEY.** Christopher…

*(**HONEY** goes through the bags too. They're not there.)*

**CHRISTOPHER.** We could go back to the ship and –

**HONEY.** It'll be long gone by now.

What are we going to –

**CHRISTOPHER.** I'm so sorry…

…

I am really sorry.

…

Are you angry?

*(Long silence.)*

> (**HONEY** *looks around: at where they are.*)
>
> (*She gathers their things.*)

**HONEY.** We need to stick to the schedule.

**CHRISTOPHER.** But we don't have any –

**HONEY.** We're here aren't we? I didn't think we'd even make it this far, I was so sure that 'They' would stop us but – we're in Antarctica! So we keep going. Until we find the edge of the world.

**CHRISTOPHER.** But we can't record any of it, can't tell people what / we've –

**HONEY.** We'll just have to see it for ourselves and hope that they believe us.

> (**HONEY** *goes on ahead.*)
>
> (**CHRISTOPHER** *stays behind.*)
>
> (*A moment.*)
>
> (**CHRISTOPHER** *checks* **HONEY** *isn't looking.*)
>
> (*Then, very quickly, he takes the cameras from a hiding place and buries them away deep in his bag.*)
>
> ,
>
> ,
>
> ,
>
> (**HONEY** *and* **CHRISTOPHER** *making their way across Antarctica, pulling their sled behind them.*)

Look at those mountains!

**CHRISTOPHER.** They're huge.

**HONEY.** The air is so fresh, isn't it?

**CHRISTOPHER.** It doesn't smell of anything.

**HONEY.** I like it.

**CHRISTOPHER.** Bloody hell, it's cold…

**HONEY.** How far have we come?

**CHRISTOPHER.** *(Checking the compass.)* A few miles.

**HONEY.** How many?

**CHRISTOPHER.** Two.

**HONEY.** Only two?

**CHRISTOPHER.** It's not a bad thing to take our time. Like you said, the terrain here's changing… there could be anything up ahead.

> (**HONEY** *sees something behind them, turns around: nothing there.*)

What is it?

**HONEY.** Nothing.

**HONEY.** What do you fancy for dinner tonight?

**CHRISTOPHER.** A roast chicken and a hot toddy.

**HONEY.** It's butter, biscuits or freeze-dried baked beans.

**CHRISTOPHER.** Like an arrow through my heart.

**HONEY.** We need butter for the calories.

**CHRISTOPHER.** What do you think roast penguin tastes like?

**HONEY.** We're not roasting a penguin!

**CHRISTOPHER.** What do you think it tastes like though?

**HONEY.** Chicken, everything tastes like –

(**HONEY** *sees it again.*)

**CHRISTOPHER.** What is it, what do you see?

**HONEY.** I said, it's nothing.

**CHRISTOPHER.** We can't hide things from each other, not out here.

**HONEY.** I thought I saw something, that's all.

**CHRISTOPHER.** Something?

**HONEY.** Someone.

**CHRISTOPHER.** (*Looking around.*) There's no one.

Do you see them now?

**HONEY.** We're alone aren't we? You just said so. We can see for miles…

**CHRISTOPHER.** IS THERE ANYBODY OUT THERE?

(*Nothing.*)

**HONEY.** See?

(**HONEY** *sets off in front of* **CHRISTOPHER** *again.*)

(*Then: a big crack of ice.*)

(*The ground opens up under* **HONEY**'s *feet.*)

(*She falls forward.*)

(**CHRISTOPHER** *catches her: pulling her back, just in time.*)

(*They lie on the ground for a moment together, in a heap.*)

**CHRISTOPHER.** What was that?

**HONEY.** The ice…it just fell away…

**CHRISTOPHER**.  You have to be careful.

**HONEY**.  I was being careful!

Sorry, you saved my –

**CHRISTOPHER**.  It's nothing.

**HONEY**.  It was like the ground just opened up and…

**CHRISTOPHER**.  It's okay I've got you.

Bloody hell, this place…

…

**HONEY**.  *(Getting up and brushes herself down.)*

**CHRISTOPHER**.  Shouldn't we – you've had a shock.

**HONEY**.  It's fine.

**CHRISTOPHER**.  But you almost –

**HONEY**.  But I didn't.

**CHRISTOPHER**.  Shouldn't we stop, rest, I don't know.

**HONEY**.  We need to make the most of these conditions, break a bit more ground before the weather changes.

,

,

,

*(The wind is picking up. And it's starting to get cold…)*

*(It's slow going.)*

How far have we come?

**CHRISTOPHER**.  Half a mile.

**HONEY**.  That can't be right…

**CHRISTOPHER.** We should put up the tent.

**HONEY.** A bit further.

*(The wind gets stronger.)*

,

,

,

*(The wind is howling now.)*

*(They can barely move.)*

We should put up the tent.

**CHRISTOPHER.** WHAT?

**HONEY.** PUT UP THE TENT!

**CHRISTOPHER.** I CAN'T HEAR YOU.

**HONEY.** TENT!

*(**CHRISTOPHER** gives a big thumbs up.)*

*(They try to put the tent up. It's a struggle –)*

**CHRISTOPHER.** HOLD IT STILL.

**HONEY.** I'M TRYING

WHERE DOES THIS –

**CHRISTOPHER.** WHAT?

**HONEY.** THIS. WHERE DOES IT –

**CHRISTOPHER.** YOU HAVE TO HOLD IT STILL.

**HONEY.** I CAN'T! THE WIND –

*(They try to get to the tent up – it blows away.)*

*(They try again: it blows away.)*

*(They get the tent up, finally and get inside.)*

*(The sound of the wind dies down a little.)*

My hands are burning.

**CHRISTOPHER.** Can I?

*(He takes **HONEY**'s hand in his, takes off her glove, and blows on her fingers to warm them up.)*

Any better?

**HONEY.** A bit.

*(He kisses her.)*

**CHRISTOPHER.** You're freezing.

**HONEY.** I feel great.

**CHRISTOPHER.** You know what the best thing for hypothermia is, don't you? Skin-to-skin contact. So I'm just saying, if you ever do start to feel like you're getting too cold, my body warmth, at your service.

**HONEY.** Selfless of you.

**CHRISTOPHER.** That and a hot cup of tea.

*(He gets out the stove, lights it and starts to make them tea.)*

**HONEY.** It's amazing here, isn't it?

**CHRISTOPHER.** That's one word for it.

**HONEY.** I feel like one of the early pioneers, like Shackleton or Scott. This is what they must've felt like.

**CHRISTOPHER.** My bones hurt. I'm exhausted.

*(The wind rages outside.)*

**CHRISTOPHER.** Hope that dies down a bit before we have to set off again.

**HONEY.** You know what they say: if you don't like the weather in Antarctica, wait five minutes.

**CHRISTOPHER.** You don't really want to be like Scott, do you?

**HONEY.** Why not?

**CHRISTOPHER.** Didn't he die a horrible death?

**HONEY.** I don't think it was so horrible.

**CHRISTOPHER.** Dying from scurvy or whatever they died from back then? Freezing to death and starving.

**HONEY.** I think there are worst places to die than Antarctica, in the pursuit of truth.

**CHRISTOPHER.** No thank you. I want a nice comfortable death: fall asleep when I'm ninety-nine in my own bed, grandkids next door... Peaceful. But dying here? What could be worse than that?

**HONEY.** There are worse ways to –

**CHRISTOPHER.** You don't really think that?

Well I think it's selfish – a selfish way to – what could be worse than –

(*HONEY looks at CHRISTOPHER.*)

...

Sorry.

**HONEY.** What's got into you?

**CHRISTOPHER.** I don't know...

**HONEY.** You're finding it tough out / here.

**CHRISTOPHER.** It's not just me, anyone would. And today...almost losing you, I –

**HONEY.** I'm fine – look at me!

**CHRISTOPHER.** You're more than fine. You're in your element out here. It's beautiful to see.

**HONEY.** It'll get easier.

**CHRISTOPHER.** When will that be?

**HONEY.** You're not regretting it are you? Coming here.

**CHRISTOPHER.** No, but you have to admit, this place…it's not natural. No smells – there's no green, anywhere… I miss trees, don't you? And the scale of it all, it makes me feel so…

**HONEY.** It'll all be worth it when we find the edge of the world.

**CHRISTOPHER.** You really think we will?

**HONEY.** I know we will.

**CHRISTOPHER.** Now we're actually here, it feels…

**HONEY.** It's 'Them' Christopher. 'They' put things in place to stop us from finding the edge but I know it's here and I know you do too.

**CHRISTOPHER.** Yes. Sorry I don't know why I'm… probably just tired.

**HONEY.** It's been a long day. We need to get some proper rest.

*(The wind outside has stopped. The sun is beating down on their tent.)*

**CHRISTOPHER.** It's not natural this, sleeping while the sun's out.

*(She turns away from him.)*

Sweet dreams.

*(**CHRISTOPHER** watches **HONEY** for a moment. He thinks about holding her, but decides against it.)*

*(He's wide awake.)*

*(He watches **HONEY** sleeping.)*

,

,

,

*(They set off.)*

*(The sun circles around them.)*

,

,

,

How far have we –

**HONEY**. A mile and a half...

**CHRISTOPHER**. But –

**HONEY**. We've covered more ground than yesterday.

**CHRISTOPHER**. It doesn't feel like it...

*(**HONEY** sees something behind them.)*

I'm hungry.

**HONEY**. You're always hungry.

**CHRISTOPHER**. I need to eat something real. A roast. Two kinds of potatoes... Not another stick of butter...

You saw it again, didn't you?

**HONEY.** Hello?

*(They look around them.)*

**CHRISTOPHER.** There's no one. Nothing for miles…

**HONEY.** What if it's 'Them'? What if 'They're' following us.

**CHRISTOPHER.** I'd be able to see 'Them' too, wouldn't I?

**HONEY.** It feels so real, but then I turn around and –

**CHRISTOPHER.** This place is enough to send anyone crazy. Take for example, that: I'm sure I've seen that before.

**HONEY.** It's a lump of ice, it looks just like all the / other –

**CHRISTOPHER.** No, I've definitely seen it before.

**HONEY.** How can you possibly know?

**CHRISTOPHER.** Because it looks like a penguin. Those are the eyes, and there's the beak.

I think we're going in circles.

**HONEY.** We can't be.

**CHRISTOPHER.** How do you know that? It all looks the same…

**HONEY.** We can't lose it out here, we have to keep it together.

,

,

,

*(They put up their tent.)*

*(They eat.)*

*(**HONEY** sleeps, **CHRISTOPHER** is wide awake.)*

*(He watches her.)*

*(They set off again.)*

(**HONEY** *sees something.*)

*(Turns around.)*

*(Nothing and no one there.)*

*(They put up their tent.)*

*(Sleep, eat, repeat.)*

*(The sun circles around them.)*

*(Until…)*

,

,

,

*(A white out.)*

**CHRISTOPHER.** We're lost.

**HONEY.** We can't be…

**CHRISTOPHER.** We have no idea where we are. And we can't see a fucking thing.

(**HONEY** *checks the compass, turns. Checks the compass again. Hits it.*)

Hey –

**HONEY.** It's not working. It just points south in every direction.

**CHRISTOPHER.** Let me see.

*(**HONEY** hands the compass to him. He looks at it. Hits it.)*

It's definitely not working.

**HONEY.** Remember what Nigel West said? Compasses stop working when you get near the wall so it must just mean we're close.

**CHRISTOPHER.** *(Harsh.)* What it means is that our compass is frozen, just like everything else in this Godforsaken place.

Sorry. I haven't been sleeping… can't get used to all this daylight.

*(**HONEY** tries to get their bearings.)*

That, there.

**HONEY.** What?

**CHRISTOPHER.** It's that lump of ice again!

**HONEY.** It's not the same.

**CHRISTOPHER.** It is!

**HONEY.** It's impossible, we're not going / in –

**CHRISTOPHER.** We can't know that because everything, everywhere is white.

**HONEY.** This'll pass soon and we'll be able to get our bearings / again and –

**CHRISTOPHER.** What if it doesn't?

**HONEY.** It will.

**CHRISTOPHER.** You can't know that.

**HONEY.** If you don't like the weather in Antarctica –

**CHRISTOPHER.** Wait five minutes, I know. But it's not getting any better.

**HONEY.** So what do you propose we do?

**CHRISTOPHER.** I say we wait for whatever this is to – like you said, and then maybe…

**HONEY.** …

**CHRISTOPHER.** We've made it all the way here and / it's –

**HONEY.** We haven't made it to the ice wall, to the edge –

**CHRISTOPHER.** But we can't document it properly, even if we do. We don't have the cameras, no one will believe us.

**HONEY.** Whose fault is that?

**CHRISTOPHER.** Good explorers know when to turn back.

**HONEY.** We're not turning back.

**CHRISTOPHER.** I want to go home.

**HONEY.** I'm not just going to give up. I've worked hard for this.

**CHRISTOPHER.** It's not just up to you, is it? And, by the way, it's not giving up. You almost died once. There could be anything up ahead, crevasses which we won't even see –

**HONEY.** We're so close, I can feel it…

**CHRISTOPHER.** Are we?

**HONEY.** Yes. It's here. I know it is.

**CHRISTOPHER.** Do you really believe that?

**HONEY.** Of course I – Why, don't you?

*(A low rumble of ice.)*

**CHRISTOPHER.** …

It's all I've thought about for so long. The true Earth. It was the only thing that really made sense to me

– finding it after I lost Charlotte, it saved me. But now we're actually here...

**HONEY**. We knew it wasn't going to be easy – 'They' are way more powerful than we are. I think you're afraid –

**CHRISTOPHER**. Yes, I'm afraid, I'm fucking terrified! Look at where we are. Being scared is the only logical response!

**HONEY**. We just have to keep going and –

**CHRISTOPHER**. I thought you wanted to come to Antarctica. I didn't think you really believed in it this much...

**HONEY**. How could you say that?

**CHRISTOPHER**. Just look around us! How can anyone be in control of this?

**HONEY**. So what – suddenly you don't believe any of it now?

**CHRISTOPHER**. I'm just not certain anymore.

**HONEY**. Then what was the point, in all this?

**CHRISTOPHER**. We found each other isn't that enough?

**HONEY**. I thought it was bigger than just...

*(Another rumble of ice – louder this time.)*

You said 'after.'

**CHRISTOPHER**. Huh?

**HONEY**. 'After' you lost Charlotte, the true Earth saved you.

**CHRISTOPHER**. Yes.

**HONEY**. You told me Louise left you. Took Charlotte away from you, because you believed in all of this...

**CHRISTOPHER.** That's right – she left me. Stopped me seeing Charlotte because of –

**HONEY.** Did she?

**CHRISTOPHER.** ...

**HONEY.** Leave you, or...?

**CHRISTOPHER.** ...Well...

I was the one who left.

...

I should've told you before.

**HONEY.** You shouldn't have have lied.

**CHRISTOPHER.** It was more complicated than... I can explain.

**HONEY.** Explain, then.

**CHRISTOPHER.** I was scared. I was much younger, immature. I felt trapped and I'm not proud of it, but it crushed me, the responsibility, the love that I felt for – until I couldn't take it anymore and...

I did try to go back. But Louise wasn't having it. She'd moved on. Didn't want to upset Charlotte so...

I know I should've told you, but none of this changes how I feel about you –

> *(The rumbling turns to a loud crack of ice beneath them.)*

What was...

> *(The white-out has lifted. Suddenly they can see where they are: on the edge of a giant crevasse.)*

I knew it. A crevasse, right here! Didn't I say?

(**CHRISTOPHER** *looks over the edge.*)

Bloody hell, that's deep...

At least the weather has cleared, we can get our bearings, make it back.

**HONEY**. I'm not going back.

**CHRISTOPHER**. I've been where you are now. I needed something to hold on to, but nothing ever fills the / hole.

**HONEY**. You didn't lose Charlotte, you abandoned her.

**CHRISTOPHER**. Don't say that, I lost everything / for –

**HONEY**. I lost Sadie. She's dead, it wasn't a choice I made. I can't ever get her back. Yes the world is awful, people are awful, but you think you're the victim? Look at you, you don't know a fucking thing.

**CHRISTOPHER**. I know what this is really about.

**HONEY**. It's about the truth. It's always been about uncovering / the –

**CHRISTOPHER**. I think it's about what happened to / her.

**HONEY**. It's about what's real. I don't care if you come with me, or / not.

**CHRISTOPHER**. I'm real, me! And we need each other out here. You can't just run away / from –

**HONEY**. I'm going to find it.

**CHRISTOPHER**. Running isn't going to make the pain go away. And it's too dangerous to keep going on your own. Sadie wouldn't want you to –

**HONEY**. How do you know what Sadie would've wanted?

**CHRISTOPHER**. She loved you, I know she did. Even at the end.

**HONEY.** How do you know that? How could you possibly know that?

**CHRISTOPHER.** Because she told me.

*(Long beat.)*

**HONEY.** Told you?

**CHRISTOPHER.** Yes.

**HONEY.** How?

**CHRISTOPHER.** We were talking.

**HONEY.** Talking?

**CHRISTOPHER.** On a forum.

**HONEY.** A –

**CHRISTOPHER.** At first, and then, um. We met up.

**HONEY.** How many times?

**CHRISTOPHER.** A couple of –

**HONEY.** How many.

**CHRISTOPHER.** Four. Maybe…

**HONEY.** She didn't say anything about…

**CHRISTOPHER.** You weren't speaking to her, were you?

**HONEY.** So that day, the day of her…

You followed me?

**CHRISTOPHER.** It was such a tragedy. I wanted to pay my respects, it just felt like the right thing to – I stood at the back. You looked so much like her… And when you slipped out, I… I wasn't planning to come and talk to you at the bar, I wanted to make sure you were okay but it just sort of…

**HONEY.** Then it wasn't chance or coincidence or fate. You tricked me.

**CHRISTOPHER.** It wasn't like that.

**HONEY.** I thought you were…that we…

Why didn't you tell me you knew her?

**CHRISTOPHER.** I didn't trick you and I know I should've told you –

**HONEY.** Did you sleep with her?

**CHRISTOPHER.** Of course not.

**HONEY.** Did you love her? Oh my God, Christopher –

**CHRISTOPHER.** We were friends, that's all. Like I said, we just talked. She was going through a lot and I was there for her. I thought you'd be happy.

**HONEY.** Happy?

**CHRISTOPHER.** Not happy, but – just that I knew her. It's like knowing another part of you. You're brilliant, a shining person, just like she was. And the darkness inside you, she had a darkness like that. She told me all about your childhood, how she was the one who practically raised you / how –

**HONEY.** You prayed on me. You groomed me, you probably groomed her too –

**CHRISTOPHER.** It wasn't like that.

**HONEY.** Her treatment…

Did you encourage her?

**CHRISTOPHER.** I understood, when no one else did – when she felt so alone and I showed her the true Earth and it helped her, just like it's helped / you –

**HONEY.** I felt sorry for you.

**CHRISTOPHER.** Don't say that.

**HONEY.** You seemed so sad. A lonely scared little man building models in your basement. But you – you –

**CHRISTOPHER**. I wasn't sad I was certain, like her. That's why you were drawn to me. I've wanted to tell you for so long but I didn't know how... we belong together, we do, and whatever you think of me, we need each other out here, if we're going to make it back.

*(**CHRISTOPHER** moves towards **HONEY**.)*

**HONEY**. Stay away from me.

**CHRISTOPHER**. I'm not going to hurt you. I love you. And I know you love me too.

**HONEY**. You're not who I thought you were.

**CHRISTOPHER**. Don't say that – please – nothing's changed.

**HONEY**. Fucking hell Christopher I spent her life insurance money on this.

**CHRISTOPHER**. Coming here was your idea.

**HONEY**. And you let me and you were lying to me this whole – about everything.

**CHRISTOPHER**. You're making it sound like – I told you, it wasn't a lie.

**HONEY**. The opposite of truth is lies.

**CHRISTOPHER**. I'm telling you the truth now. This is all of it, the whole truth. I'm not a bad person. I wasn't trying to –

**HONEY**. How can I trust anything you say?

**CHRISTOPHER**. I'm not the only one who lied. There are things you didn't tell me.

**HONEY**. That's not the same.

**CHRISTOPHER**. I know why you feel so guilty, but you don't have to.

**HONEY**. You don't know / anything.

**CHRISTOPHER**. You sent Sadie that post, but it's okay, you did the right thing –

**HONEY**. Shut UP.

**CHRISTOPHER**. We're the same, Honey.

**HONEY**. We're not / the –

**CHRISTOPHER**. And we can still go home now and have a beautiful life together.

Please?

I need you to believe me. I know how it looks, but it wasn't malicious – it all just spun out of...

Honey, please? Believe me.

Please, believe me.

Believe me, Honey. Please?

> (**CHRISTOPHER** *holds out his hand to her.*)
>
> (**HONEY** *looks at him.*)
>
> (*Then she screams and runs at him.*)
>
> (*They fall.*)
>
> (*The sound of ice, breaking.*)
>
> —
>
> (*The crevasse.*)
>
> (*Dripping, creaking, echoing, darkness.*)
>
> (**HONEY**, *alone, with her eyes closed.*)
>
> (*The ice moves around her.*)
>
> (*The blue light is brighter and closer now.*)

*(Then.)*

*(**HONEY** jolts awake, suddenly, like falling.)*

*(She looks around...)*

**HONEY.** Christopher?

*(Nothing.)*

*(His bag is still there. She opens it: pulls out various items until she finds...)*

*(The cameras that he hid from her.)*

*(Another lie.)*

*(The blue light is even brighter.)*

*(**HONEY** sees it.)*

*(Starts to crawl towards it.)*

*(Dragging herself with all her strength through a hole in the ice and out into...)*

*(Bright sunlight.)*

*(She lies therefor a second. Feels the gentle warmth of sun on her face.)*

*(She pulls herself up. Starts to walk. It's slow going.)*

*(She sees a door on the horizon: walks towards it. Opens it.)*

*(Wetherspoons.)*

*(In the background, we hear **HONEY** and **CHRISTOPHER**'s voices on the day they met, like a low rumble.)*

*(Or maybe it is just the sound of moving ice.)*

**VOICE**. Good evening Honey.

**HONEY**. Who said that –

**VOICE**. Where are you?

**HONEY**. I...

**VOICE**. Where do you think you are?

**HONEY**. I thought I was in Antarctica / but...

**VOICE**. And where is it you think you are going?

**HONEY**. To the edge of the world.

**VOICE**. *(Laughs.)*

**HONEY**. Can I have something to drink?

**VOICE**. We've got – frozen beer? Frozen apple juice? A hot toddy?

**HONEY**. Water.

**VOICE**. We're not that kind of establishment here, I'm afraid.

**HONEY**. Please, I'm so thirsty...

**NIGEL**. "The truth can withstand investigation."

*(**HONEY** spins around.)*

*(Sees.)*

**HONEY**. Nigel West.

**NIGEL**. Guilty.

**HONEY**. How did you get here?

**NIGEL.** I got your DM. It was quite a trek, but I needed to see this for myself. I have to say I'm impressed that you made it this far. I thought you'd be dead by now.

**HONEY.** Can you help me? Which way do I go?

**NIGEL.** Where is it you're trying to end up?

**HONEY.** The edge of the world.

**NIGEL.** It's almost heartbreaking how much you still believe it...

**HONEY.** I believe it because it's real –

**NIGEL.** ...

**HONEY.** But...all your posts and videos...

**NIGEL.** Oh don't look at me like that. I saw a gap in the market and I filled it.

**HONEY.** So you're a liar, too, just like him...

**NIGEL.** Lighten up! I'm a storyteller.

**HONEY.** What's the difference?

**NIGEL.** What does it matter? People need stories. And they love to be deceived! Take you, for example. Before me, your life was sad, lonely, painful, meaningless. Working a pointless job you hated, struggling to make ends meet, no family to speak of, the only person you ever really loved, your sister, needlessly dead... I gave you a story and it helped you. I made you the hero. Made you feel powerful!

**HONEY.** It wasn't just / a –

**NIGEL.** Everything is a story. Our governments, our legal systems, economics, institutions, corporations – all of them, fictional stories that only exist because we believe in them. But these stories are losing their power. The world as we know it is crumbling. The old order is over.

Where you see chaos, I see opportunity. An ordinary man with a phone can speak to the whole world. That's truth; that's democracy, that's freedom. I'm a visionary. The world is an exciting place right now – it's all ripe for the taking.

Of course, there will be casualties. We are all just animals in the end, driven by our baser instincts; fear, jealousy, rage, hate.... and every good story needs a villain. Someone to blame, someone to hate.

Them, The Illuminati, the Secret Cabal, the immigrants, the Islamists, the leftists, the lizards, the Jews... They're hiding things from you! They're replacing you! Lying to you! Stealing your jobs! Stealing your money! Fucking your children!

(**NIGEL** *laughs, heartily*)

It is really very easy to make people hate one other. And when they do... divide and conquer: the world is yours.

**HONEY.** How does any of this help anyone but you?

**NIGEL.** Sweet, naive Honey. The world is what it is. And people are stupid – easily led. It's not my fault that I could tell them the sky was pink, even if it was blue, and they'd still believe me.

**HONEY.** You can't just lie to people.

**NIGEL.** On the contrary: to destroy things, you can lie all you want.

**HONEY.** I thought you were different...

**NIGEL.** Just another disappointing, self-interested animal, I'm afraid. Pinch me, see? Flesh and bone.

(**NIGEL** *pinches* **HONEY**.)

**HONEY.** Ouch.

**NIGEL.** You've pissed yourself, by the way.

*(They snap back to Antarctica. White, everywhere...)*

**HONEY**. I don't believe you.

**NIGEL**. Now you don't believe me?

**HONEY**. It has to be real...it's the truth –

**NIGEL**. My truth or yours?

**HONEY**. There is only one.

**NIGEL**. Truth is messy. It's unbelievable. It's a bag of contradictions. It's infinite.

*(**NIGEL WEST** disappears.)*

**HONEY**. Wait!

WAIT!

*(Nothing.)*

Which way? Which way do I...

**VOICE**. South.

**HONEY**. Which way is south?

**VOICE**. Every way is south.

*(She hesitates. She picks a direction, starts to walk.)*

I wouldn't go that way if I were you...

*(She picks another direction.)*

Or that way...

**HONEY**. Why not? What happens if I –

This is stupid. You're talking to yourself. Just...keep it together.

*(She sets off.)*

*(And then...behind her.)*

*(A giant **PENGUIN** appears.)*

*(It starts to follow her.)*

*(She turns around.)*

No...

*(She keeps walking.)*

*(Turns around again.)*

*(Sees the **PENGUIN**, it's definitely still there.)*

That's not possible.

**PENGUIN.** What's not possible?

**HONEY.** A giant talking penguin.

**PENGUIN.** I have a name. It's José.

*(**HONEY** closes her eyes and opens them again.)*

I've been following you.

**HONEY.** Just ignore /it...

**PENGUIN.** And watching you.

**HONEY.** You're losing your mind, that's all that's happening.

**PENGUIN.** Can I tell you a story?

**HONEY.** No!

**PENGUIN.** Why not?

**HONEY.** Because you're not real, you're in my head.

**PENGUIN.** That doesn't make me any less true.

*(The **PENGUIN** pinches her.)*

**HONEY.** Ow!

**PENGUIN.** See?

> (**HONEY** *tries to walk away, but the* **PENGUIN** *follows her.*)

Where are you going?

**HONEY.** To find the edge.

**PENGUIN.** Let me come too?

**HONEY.** I want to be alone.

**PENGUIN.** It's not natural to be alone. We are social animals.

At least let me tell you the story. Go on…it's about you.

Don't you want to know what happens?

**HONEY.** I don't care what happens.

**PENGUIN.** Don't you want to know it ends?

**HONEY.** I'm dead aren't I? That's how it ends.

**PENGUIN.** Your guess is as good as mine.

**HONEY.** Wouldn't it have hurt?

**PENGUIN.** Dying is a lot less painful than living. Then again, it's the pain that reminds us we're alive.

**HONEY.** I just want it to stop…

**PENGUIN.** Have you tried heroin?

**HONEY.** Have you?!

**PENGUIN.** *(Not a no.)* It's not a long term solution. And even then, the pain will never just stop. Take Christopher, for instance.

**HONEY.** He's dangerous.

**PENGUIN**. You believed what you wanted to believe: chose the best story and made the narrative fit. But you must admit, it's been magical.

**HONEY**. Magical?

**PENGUIN**. Look where you are!

**HONEY**. He lied to me.

**PENGUIN**. You lied to him too, didn't you?

>(**HONEY** *stops.*)
>
>(**PENGUIN** *claps his flippers together and the music stops, and the house lights come up.*)
>
>(**HONEY** *suddenly sees everything: the lights above her, the stage, all of it.*)

**PENGUIN**. Where are you?

**HONEY**. I'm...it looks like a studio or –

**PENGUIN**. You're in a theatre.

**HONEY**. Does that mean...

**PENGUIN**. The world as you know it is all just a simulation, all an illusion.

**HONEY**. Then...it's all...just like *The Truman Show*!

But then...who's in charge? Who's pulling the –

**PENGUIN**. We are.

**HONEY**. By we you mean...

**PENGUIN**. You were right to be scared of us.

**HONEY**. You've got to be fucking kidding me.

>(**HONEY** *looks out at the audience: sees them for the first time.*)

**HONEY**. They're all penguins...

**PENGUIN**. (Yes)

**HONEY**. And they've all just been been sitting here this whole time watching me?

**PENGUIN**. We are everywhere. We have infiltrated your institutions: the BBC, the royal family, NASA, the government... we have put penguins in all the highest offices of state. We can shape shift, appear just like you. King Charles is a penguin. The president and the prime minister are penguins. The Queen was a penguin – but that was clear to anyone who cared to look...

...

**HONEY**. I don't understand... Why? Why did you bring me here?

Why am I here?

Tell me the truth!

**PENGUIN**. I'll tell you my story now.

Once upon a time, a woman called Sadie discovers a small, hard lump in her left breast. She has never been ill before, she rarely even gets a cold– so when the diagnosis comes, she can hardly believe it.

That's when her sister Honey – who has always distrusted doctors, always been sceptical of mainstream medicine – sends her a post about an alternative cure. It doesn't sound like much but Sadie reads this post and it plants a seed of doubt within her. And that seed of doubt: it grows and grows...

Until Sadie becomes convinced that the doctors are hiding things from her... that the treatment they want her to have will kill her. Soon she has lost herself down the rabbit hole. She is so far down it, that she can no longer be reached, not even by her sister, who feels so guilty and is so angry with her for dying without a fight that she stops speaking to her in the final months before her death.

The irony is that Sadie is doing all of this because she doesn't want to die. She doesn't want to suffer. But, by the time she realises her mistake, it is too late. She suffers, terribly. And then she dies.

**HONEY.** *(Crying.)* I thought I was helping her…

**PENGUIN.** Not a very nice story, was it?

Here's a better one.

Once upon a time a woman called Sadie is diagnosed with cancer. She is scared, everything feels so out of her control and in this storm of uncertainty and fear, she desperately searches for something solid to anchor herself to.

She spends more and more time scrolling online and, pushed to it by internet algorithms driven by profit and fear, she refuses the treatment that the doctors are offering her. It is not Honey's fault that Sadie makes the choice she does. There is nothing Honey can do to change Sadie's path.

Which one is true?

**HONEY.** You know which one…

**PENGUIN.** I don't believe either of them.

**HONEY.** I don't know what to believe anymore…

**PENGUIN.** Good, doubt is good. It's the only truth, when you think about it.

**HONEY.** What happens? How does it end?

*(Suddenly, the lights go down again and the **PENGUIN** disappears.)*

**HONEY.** How does it end?

> *(**HONEY** is completely alone.)*

*(She looks out in the direction of the audience, trying to make them out, but she can't see them anymore.)*

*(We snap back to Antarctica.)*

Hello?

Are you…

Is anybody…

*(She's alone.)*

*(The wind is raging. The sky is black She's freezing, holding herself for warmth.)*

Go on, then. Get it over with.

*(Just the freezing wind.)*

Is that the best you can do?

…

I said – IS THAT THE BEST YOU CAN DO?

*(Nothing. She is completely alone. Shouting into the void.)*

Please? I've had enough…

*(**HONEY** starts to laugh. A laugh that builds until it feels like crying. For the first time, **HONEY** surrenders – to the chaos, to the pain. Just as, somewhere else… **CHRISTOPHER** begins to wake up.)*

*(A bigger laugh.)*

I'M READY! DO YOUR WORST!!

*(But then.)*

*(There's a break in the clouds.)*

*(The wind stops howling.)*

*(A flash of sun.)*

*(And for a moment, it looks as if it is raining gold dust all around her.)*

*(In fact, it is the ice crystals in the air illuminated by the sun.)*

*(**HONEY** drinks it in, lets the gold dust fall on her face.)*

*(**CHRISTOPHER** sees the gold dust all around him...)*

*(They enjoy it for a moment.)*

*(It really is magical.)*

*(Then.)*

*(A crack of ice, the biggest yet.)*

*(**HONEY** and **CHRISTOPHER** see each other.)*

*(They look around.)*

You...

**CHRISTOPHER**. Where am I?

**HONEY**. Are you real?

**CHRISTOPHER**. I think so...are you?

**HONEY**. I don't know anymore.

...

Where've they gone?

**CHRISTOPHER.** Who?

**HONEY.** *(Looking at the audience.)* There were…where did they go?

**CHRISTOPHER.** I was dead…and then…you. And now we're here and…

I'm so sorry about everything… all the lies, it all just got so out of control –

**HONEY.** It's a lot of lies Christopher.

**CHRISTOPHER.** I know.

*(He starts to cry.)*

**HONEY.** What do we do now?

**CHRISTOPHER.** Get the hell out of here and never come back this terrible place as long as we live?

*(The light is changing. The sun is setting.)*

*(Then **HONEY** sees something up ahead…)*

**HONEY.** Oh my god…

**CHRISTOPHER.** What?

**HONEY.** Over there…is that…?

**CHRISTOPHER.** It can't be…

**HONEY.** It is, it's right there. Look at it, it's –

**CHRISTOPHER.** Does that mean…

**HONEY.** We made it! We actually…

*(**HONEY** laughs with pure joy.)*

I don't believe it…

**CHRISTOPHER.** I feel…

**HONEY.** Heat. All over…

**CHRISTOPHER.** It's so warm. It's…

**HONEY.** The most beautiful thing I've ever…

**CHRISTOPHER.** The sun…

**HONEY.** Falling over the edge of the world…

**CHRISTOPHER.** And the sky! Do you see that? It's…

**HONEY.** Pink.

>*(They laugh.)*

>*(The sound of ice cracking and water rushing.)*

>*(Lights down.)*

## End of Play

www.ingramcontent.com/pod-product-compliance
Ingram Content Group UK Ltd.
Pitfield, Milton Keynes, MK11 3LW, UK
UKHW010838181125
465148UK00005B/26